*Student
Teaching
in
Physical
Education*

STUDENT TEACHING IN PHYSICAL EDUCATION

by

IRWIN ROSENSTEIN

and

GERALD J. HASE

PRENTICE-HALL, Inc., Englewood Cliffs, N.J.

GV
362
.R6
1971

© 1971 by Prentice-Hall, Inc., Englewood Cliffs, N.J.

All rights reserved. No part of this book may be reproduced in any form or by any means without permission in writing from the publisher.

13-857862-1

Library of Congress Catalog Card Number: 74-131997

Printed in the United States of America

Current Printing (last number):

10 9 8 7 6 5 4 3 2 1

PRENTICE-HALL INTERNATIONAL, INC., London
PRENTICE-HALL OF AUSTRALIA, PTY. LTD., Sydney
PRENTICE-HALL OF CANADA, LTD., Toronto
PRENTICE-HALL OF INDIA PRIVATE LIMITED, New Delhi
PRENTICE-HALL OF JAPAN, INC., Tokyo

Contents

part I   STUDENT TEACHING: why and with whom?   1

CHAPTER 1

Philosophy of Student Teaching, 3

Common Terms Used in Student Teaching, 4
Purposes, 5
What Makes a Good Student Teacher?, 7
Getting to Know the School and Community, 7
The Selection of Cooperating Schools, 9
Selected References, 11

CHAPTER 2

Roles Played by Personnel in Student Teaching, 13

The Role of the Student Teacher, 13
The Role of the Supervising Teacher, 14
The Role of the College Supervisor, 15
The Role of the Cooperating-School Administrator, 16

part II STUDENT TEACHING: how, when? 19

CHAPTER 3

Elementary and Secondary-School Class and Extra-Class Programs, 21

The Physical Education Class Program, 21
The Philosophy of Physical Education, 21
The Objectives of Physical Education, 22
Program Planning, 24
Program Activities, 25

class program: situations and analysis, 29

First Situation: Discipline by Another Teacher, 29
Second Situation: The Ballet Dancer, 30
Third Situation: Showering, 31
Fourth Situation: Dressing in Physical Education Uniform, 32
Fifth Situation: An Uncoordinated Program, 33
Sixth Situation: The National Guard, 33
Discussion Notes, 35
Personal Practice-Teaching Experience Related to Topic, 35

extra-class program: situations and analysis, 36

First Situation: Boxing, 36
Second Situation: Scholastic Eligibility, 36
Third Situation: The Football Player, 37
Fourth Situation: Unequal Intramural Teams, 38
Fifth Situation: Limiting Team Membership, 39
Discussion Notes, 41
Personal Practice-Teaching Experience Related to Topic, 41
Selected References, 42

CHAPTER 4

Swimming Pools, 45

Contributions of Swimming and Water Safety, 45
Public Interest and Support for a Swimming Pool, 46
The School Swimming Program, 47
Administration of a School Aquatics Program, 47
The Designing and Construction of Swimming Pools, 48
First Situation: Promoting a School Swimming Pool, 50
Second Situation: Financing the School Swimming Pool, 51
Third Situation: Long Hair, 52
Fourth Situation: The Location of the Pool, 53
Fifth Situation: Athlete's Foot, 54

Sixth Situation: Excusing Girl Swimmers, 55
Discussion Notes, 56
Personal Practice-Teaching Experience Related to Topic, 56
Selected References, 57

CHAPTER 5

Personnel and Scheduling, 59

Personnel, 59
Scheduling, 63
Personnel Situations and Analysis, 65
First Situation: Insufficient Staff, 65
Second Situation: Shortage of Teachers for Girls, 66
Third Situation: Shortage of Coaches, 67
Fourth Situation: The Lay Coach, 68
Fifth Situation: Shortage of Staff, 69
Sixth Situation: Supervision of Intramural Activities, 70
Discussion Notes, 72
Personal Practice-Teaching Experience Related to Topic, 72
Scheduling Situations and Analysis, 73
First Situation: Indoor Facilities, 73
Second Situation: Large Classes, 74
Third Situation: Scheduling Girls' Extracurricular Activities, 75
Fourth Situation: Age Grouping, 76
Fifth Situation: Modular Scheduling, 76
Discussion Notes, 78
Personal Practice-Teaching Experience Related to Topic, 78
Selected References, 79

CHAPTER 6

Budget, 81

Sources of Income for Public Education, 81
Financial Management in Physical Education, 82
Budgeting for Physical Education and Athletics, 82
The Budget for Interscholastic Athletics, 86
Supplies and Equipment, 87
Budget Situations and Analysis, 88
First Situation: Falling Gate Receipts, 88
Second Situation: A Trampoline, 89
Third Situation: Supplies and Equipment, 90
Fourth Situation: Laundry Equipment, 91
Fifth Situation: Unbudgeted Equipment, 92
Sixth Situation: Budget Cuts, 93
Discussion Notes, 95
Personal Practice-Teaching Experience Related to Topic, 95
Selected References, 96

CHAPTER 7

Facilities, 99

Outdoor Facilities, 109
Situations and Analysis, 115
First Situation: Limited Indoor Facilities, 115
Second Situation: Planning the Courts Area, 115
Third Situation: Gymnasium Courts, 116
Fourth Situation: Dressing Rooms and Showering Rooms, 117
Sixth Situation: Partitioning the Gymnasium, 119
Discussion Notes, 120
Personal Practice-Teaching Experience Related to Topic, 120
Selected References, 121

CHAPTER 8

Safety Aspects of Physical Education, 123

Administration, 124
Curriculum and Instruction, 124
Facilities, 125
Equipment and Supplies, 125
First Aid and Emergency Care, 126
Reporting and Investigating Accidents, 126
Situations and Analysis, 127
First Situation: Safe Playground Equipment, 127
Second Situation: An Indoor Relay Race, 128
Third Situation: Simultaneous Activities, 129
Fourth Situation: Sneakers, 130
Fifth Situation: Gymnasium Flooring, 131
Sixth Situation: Playing Football with a Handicap, 131
Discussion Notes, 133
Personal Practice-Teaching Experience Related to Topic, 133
Selected References, 134

CHAPTER 9

Legal Aspects of Physical Education, 137

Laws, Regulations, and Policies, 137
Who Pays for Accidents, 138
Legality of Waiver and Permission Slips, 140
School District Liability, 141
Situations and Analysis, 141
First Situation: Boxing, 141
Second Situation: A Crowded Gymnasium, 143
Third Situation: Difficult Gymnastics, 144
Fourth Situation: Uniforms, 144
Fifth Situation: Defective Playground Equipment, 145

CONTENTS ix

Sixth Situation: Wrestling Competition, 146
Discussion Notes, 148
Personal Practice-Teaching Experience Related to Topic, 148
Selected References, 149

CHAPTER 10

Evaluation, 151

The Purposes of Measurement and Evaluation, 152
Types of Measuring Instruments, 152
The Selection of Appropriate Tests, 153
Situations and Analysis, 154
First Situation: Criteria for Marks, 154
Second Situation: Evaluating Many Pupils, 155
Third Situation: Reporting Test Scores to Parents, 156
Fourth Situation: A Marking Plan, 157
Fifth Situation: Failing in Physical Education, 158
Sixth Situation: Physical-Fitness Tests, 159
Discussion Notes, 160
Personal Practice-Teaching Experience Related to Topic, 160
Selected References, 161

CHAPTER 11

Public Relations, 162

The Functions of Public Relations, 163
Principles of Public Relations, 164
Public-Relations Media, 165
Situations and Analysis, 167
First Situation: Star Performers, 167
Second Situation: Bulletin Boards, 168
Third Situation: A Football Film, 169
Fourth Situation: A Newspaper Story, 170
Fifth Situation: Showers, 171
Sixth Situation: A P.T.A. Talk, 171
Selected References, 172

CHAPTER 12

The Evaluation of Student Teaching, 175

A Cooperative Effort, 175
Purposes of Evaluation, 175
Principles of Evaluation, 176
Techniques of Evaluation, 176

INDEX, 201

Preface

This text was several years in the making and it was our hope that the book would help students to identify problems and to aid teachers in suggesting possible solutions.

The situations describing the problems are actual cases that have frequently occurred in many school districts. In our twenty-six years of supervision in over five hundred schools, we have been given the opportunity of having identified for us the many problems that exist in the local school districts. The problems described in this workbook are the pertinent ones that actually exist at the local level. The analyses as stated give suggested solutions that are for the most part the ideas of imaginative teachers, directors of health, physical education, and recreation, principals, and superintendents. These suggestions are more than theoretical because they are actually being conducted in schools throughout the nation.

The text-workbook has been divided into nine areas so that the teacher and student can easily identify general categories of problems. Each area contains several situations that are practical existing problems in today's elementary and secondary schools. Our listing is not meant to be all inclusive but we feel that we have described the most pertinent cases.

We trust that our years of accumulating practical problems with suggested solutions from many school personnel, "on the firing line," will aid many students with their present problems or the ones they may face in the future.

Irwin Rosenstein
Gerald J. Hase

*Student
Teaching
in
Physical
Education*

part I

STUDENT TEACHING:

why and with whom?

Philosophy of Student Teaching

CHAPTER 1

It is believed by educators that student teaching is one of the most important aspects of the professional preparation of teachers. Those responsible for designing the student-teaching program must remember that the experiences of the student teacher should be a series of activities as nearly like the real teaching situation as possible. Through many and varied experiences, opportunities should be provided for physical education student teachers to develop the ability: (1) to motivate pupils to develop and maintain good health and physical fitness; (2) to guide learners in the pursuit of knowledge and skills; (3) to prepare boys and girls to become socially competent and worthwhile citizens; and (4) to prepare pupils to assume their responsibilities in a democratic society.

It is generally recognized in the profession that there is great significance in the student-teaching experience as part of teacher preparation. Student teaching is a basic requirement for state certification and a principal prerequisite for the approval of an institution by the National Council for the Accreditation of Teacher Education.

Student teaching is the time when the student tests the knowledge and techniques he has learned in professional courses in the light of their practicality, feasibility, and effectiveness in a particular situation. This is the time that the student teacher puts into practice theories of education, along with his own ideas, so that he becomes skilled, and ready for a full-time teaching position. Since it is a time for the student teacher to practice, some educators refer to this experience as "practice teaching."

4 STUDENT TEACHING: WHY AND WITH WHOM?

In order for the student-teaching experience to be productive and worthwhile, it is essential to have the cooperation of three people: (1) the *supervising teacher*, who is a regular teacher of physical education in the school and who has been delegated by the school to supervise the student teacher; (2) the *college supervisor*, who represents the college or university and assigns and periodically supervises student teachers in schools; and (3) the *student teacher*, the focal point of both the college supervisor and the supervising teacher. He has a dual responsibility, in that he is a student at the college or university and he is teaching pupils in a school.

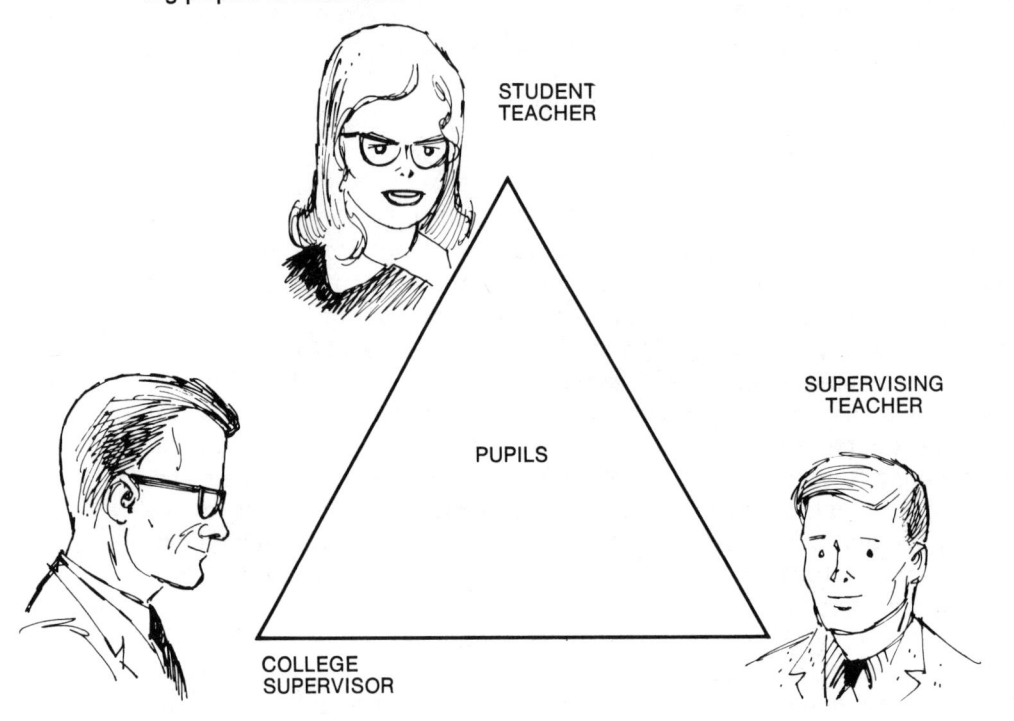

COMMON TERMS USED IN STUDENT TEACHING

Although there are no standard terms in the vocabulary for student teaching, the following terms are generally accepted by educators:

Cooperating school. An off-campus school which has appropriate facilities and personnel for professional laboratory experiences, including student teaching.

College supervisor. A member of the college faculty who has the responsibility for supervising student teachers in cooperation with the supervising teacher in the cooperating school.

Professional laboratory experience. All of the school and community activities of the student teacher which involve observation, participation, teaching, and other leadership opportunities leading to a greater understanding of the teacher's role.

Student teacher. A college student who has completed the minimum requirements for student teaching and has been assigned to a cooperating school for his professional laboratory experience.

Student teaching. A period of time when the student teacher, under the guidance of the supervising teacher and college supervisor, teaches pupils in a cooperating school.

Supervising teacher. Sometimes referred to as a *cooperating teacher* or *master teacher* in the cooperating school to whom the student teacher is assigned.

PURPOSES

The major purposes of student teaching are to provide: (1) direct opportunities of a varied nature which permit first-hand experiences with pupils; (2) a teaching situation involving problems which the future teacher has an opportunity to analyze; (3) opportunities for the student teacher to put into practice many of the theories studied in various professional preparation courses; and (4) situations where teaching skills and competencies are developed.

The objectives of student teaching in physical education, in particular, are as follows:

☐ To provide experiences in which the student teacher will work with pupils in many school situations, including the gymnasium, swimming pool, athletic field, and playground.

☐ To provide experiences which will develop the student teacher's ability to teach skills and knowledges in a variety of activities.

☐ To provide experiences which will lead the student teacher to recognize, adjust to, and make provisions for individual differences in the skills of pupils.

☐ To provide experiences in which the student teacher learns to develop the ability to handle daily class routines.

☐ To provide experiences in which the student teacher learns to evaluate pupils in terms of physical fitness, skills, knowledges, and social competence.

☐ To provide experiences which will enable the student teacher to view the school as a whole and to learn his responsibilities in carrying out administrative policies and in accomplishing the general objectives of the school program.

☐ To provide experiences which will give the student teacher an opportunity to work with pupils of all ages.

☐ To provide experiences which will stimulate the student teacher's desire for continuous professional and academic growth.

☐ To provide experiences that will enable the student teacher to develop into a well-balanced individual, a person possessing a pleasing personality and desirable personal characteristics.

☐ To help the student teacher discover, use, and appraise group processes that promote effective human relations.

☐ To provide the student teacher with opportunities for self-analysis and for the development of self-confidence.

☐ To help the student teacher to use the needs, problems, and interests of the pupils as a basis for planning, developing, and evaluating their learning experiences.

☐ To provide experiences which create an understanding of human development, both physical and mental.

☐ To provide experiences that will give the student teacher the opportunity to work with parents, teachers, and others in promoting physical education.

☐ To provide experiences that will give the student teacher the opportunity to plan units of work and to make daily lesson plans.

☐ To provide experiences in which the student teacher develops the ability to guide learning through democratic procedures.

☐ To provide experiences in which the student teacher establishes learning situations designed to develop critical thinking on the part of pupils.

☐ To provide experiences in which the student teacher has the opportunity to use many techniques of instruction and to develop his teaching skills to the point where he is competent to handle many teaching situations independently.

☐ To provide experiences in which the student teacher learns to select, use, and interpret objective data and records so as to understand and guide the pupil's growth.

☐ To provide experiences which will enable the student teacher to become familiar with professional literature, textbooks, reference materials, community resources, and teaching equipment, particularly in physical education.

☐ To provide experiences which will enable the student teacher to learn how the school and community can work together.

☐ To establish within the student teacher the feeling that he belongs to the school and has responsibilities equal to that of a full-time teacher.

WHAT MAKES A GOOD STUDENT TEACHER

It is generally agreed that a good physical education student teacher is distinguished by:

- ☐ A sincere interest in teaching as a career.
- ☐ Initiative, interest, and enthusiasm in solving problems.
- ☐ An attitude of inquiry toward everyday situations.
- ☐ A professional and mature attitude toward his work and his colleagues.
- ☐ Thorough preparation and planning for daily teaching responsibilities, including coaching.
- ☐ Willingness to read professional literature in physical education and in general education.
- ☐ Behavior that is acceptable in his school and community.
- ☐ Acceptable standards of cleanliness and neatness.
- ☐ A desire to attend and participate in school and community meetings.
- ☐ His appreciation of the chance to learn and improve his essential skills in teaching physical education.

GETTING TO KNOW THE SCHOOL AND COMMUNITY

It is very important that the student teacher become acquainted with the community in which he will reside and the school in which he will teach, if he is to become an effective member of the teaching staff. By studying the people in the local situation very carefully he can learn things which may directly affect the pupil-teacher relationship in the physical education program. It is also important that the supervising teacher create opportunities, not only in the teaching station but also in the school and community, for the student teacher to participate in school and community affairs. Often, this requires special planning because special arrangements have to be made. The supervising teacher has the responsibility for seeing that the student teacher has varied and extensive experiences outside of his regular teaching.

By participating in the total school program, the student teacher:

- ☐ Can gain greater insight into the problems and complexities of the day-to-day operation of today's schools.

8   STUDENT TEACHING: WHY AND WITH WHOM?

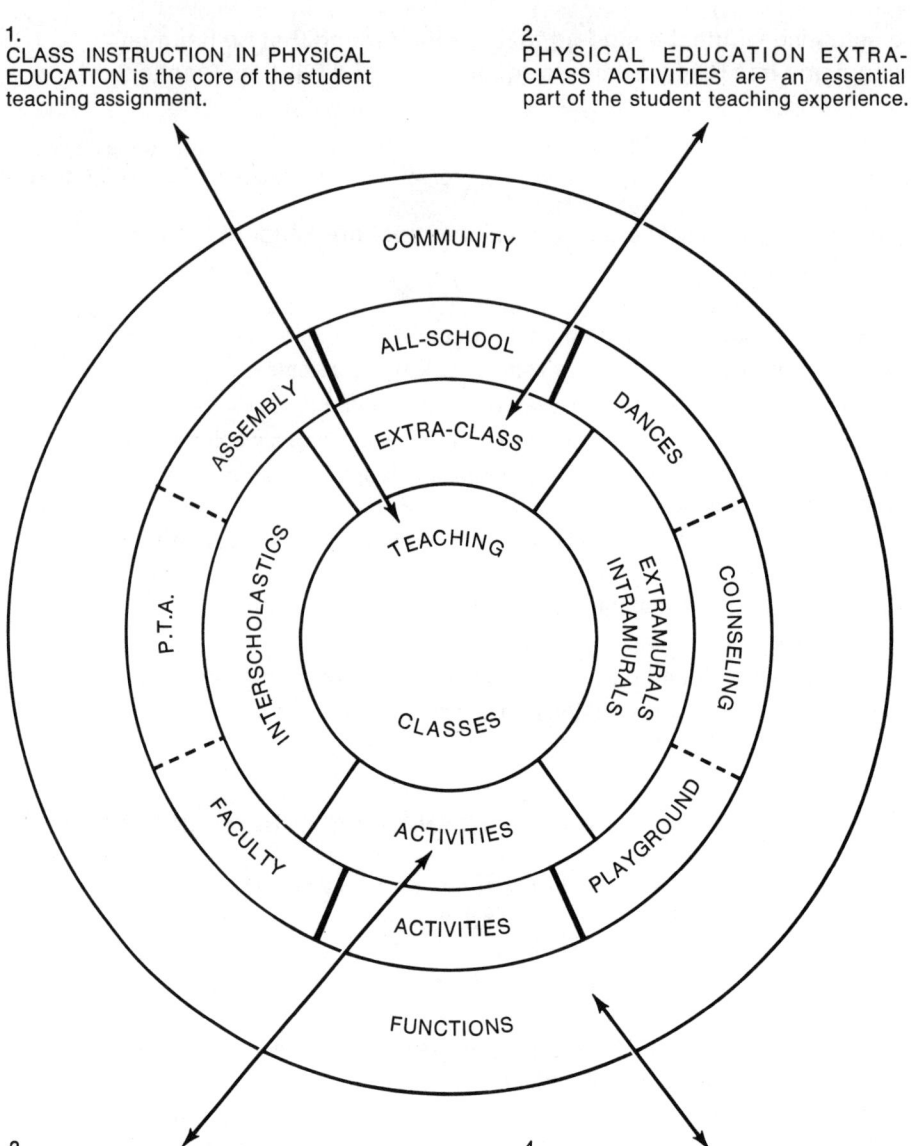

1.
CLASS INSTRUCTION IN PHYSICAL EDUCATION is the core of the student teaching assignment.

2.
PHYSICAL EDUCATION EXTRA-CLASS ACTIVITIES are an essential part of the student teaching experience.

3.
ALL-SCHOOL ACTIVITIES should give the student teacher in physical education a better understanding of the total school curriculum.

4.
COMMUNITY FUNCTIONS will give the student teacher greater insight into the community and the students he teaches.

- ☐ Will have an opportunity to meet every teacher in the school on a personal as well as a professional basis.
- ☐ Will meet and get to understand the problems of other school personnel, such as principals, guidance counselors, and custodians, as they relate to the total school program including physical education.
- ☐ Can meet with other teachers to observe and analyze different methods, techniques, and philosophies in other areas of education.
- ☐ Can develop his own social growth by being diplomatic, a good listener, and capable of expressing one's self.
- ☐ Will become better acquainted with his pupils and other pupils outside of physical education.
- ☐ Will have an opportunity to display a particular talent or skill he may possess.

Many of the values of participation in the total school program can also be attained by participation in community affairs. The student teacher who takes an active part in community activities will develop skills of a personal, social, and professional nature. However, there are certain broader benefits to be achieved, including:

- ☐ The opportunity for the student teacher to be accepted and to gain respect in the community.
- ☐ The opportunity to meet some of the parents of the children in his physical education classes.
- ☐ The opportunity to meet some of the leaders of the community.
- ☐ The opportunity to see what part community leaders have in determining school policies.
- ☐ The opportunity for interpreting the physical education program of the school to the community leaders.
- ☐ The opportunity to discuss the needs of the physical education program with members of the community.
- ☐ The opportunity to observe his pupils interact with their parents and other adults in situations outside of the school, which should give the student teacher a better understanding of his pupils.

THE SELECTION OF COOPERATING SCHOOLS

It should now be clear that one of the greatest contributions that a school can make to the future of education is to provide experiences for student teachers. Close cooperation is essential between the teacher preparation institution and the cooperating schools if these experiences

10 STUDENT TEACHING: WHY AND WITH WHOM?

are to be of greatest value, however. The cooperating schools should be carefully selected, since they are the key to a successful student-teaching experience. The following criteria should be used in selecting cooperating schools:

LEADERSHIP

School administrators and cooperating teachers should be capable of providing the most competent leadership to the student teachers. This means:

- ☐ They are interested in accepting student teachers.
- ☐ They are up-to-date.
- ☐ The school's personnel is wholesome and well-adjusted.
- ☐ The school's personnel work cooperatively with the teacher-preparation institution.
- ☐ The supervising teachers have appropriate experience and education.
- ☐ The supervising teachers participate in professional organizations and conferences.

CURRICULUM

A broad and comprehensive curriculum which provides a wide range of student-teaching experiences in physical education. This means:

- ☐ The school's program includes a wide range of activities.
- ☐ Student teachers have an opportunity to teach at all grade levels.
- ☐ The program of physical education meets the needs, interests, and abilities of the pupils.
- ☐ Appropriate changes in program are made when research indicates the need for change.
- ☐ Student teachers have opportunities to participate in physical education extra-class activities, all-school activities, and community functions.

FACILITIES

The school should have adequate facilities, equipment, and supplies for a broad program with many activities. This means:

- ☐ ·The school's outdoor and indoor physical education facilities permit the development of a comprehensive program.
- ☐ The school allows for sufficient instructional time.

☐ It has an adequate number of physical education teaching stations to accommodate the enrollment.
☐ It has a variety of facilities to take care of the many activities in the program.
☐ It has sufficient and varied enough equipment and supplies to meet the pupils' needs.

SELECTED REFERENCES

ALEXANDER, RUTH H., "How to Prevent the Student Teaching Blues," *Journal of Health, Physical Education and Recreation,* XLI (March, 1970), pp. 93–95.

BENNETT, BRUCE L., "Tell it to Mom and Dad," *Journal of Health, Physical Education and Recreation,* XXXIII (March, 1962), pp. 31, 80.

COTTON, JACK, "Teaching Experiences before Student Teaching," *Journal of Health, Physical Education and Recreation,* XXXVI (May, 1965), p. 59.

CRASE, DARRELL, "Analysis of Student Teacher Relations in Physical Education," *The Physical Educator,* XXVI (October, 1969), pp. 129–131.

FINLAYSON, ANNE, "A Consumer's Position on Teacher Preparation," *Journal of Health, Physical Education and Recreation,* XXXV (May, 1964), pp. 39, 73, 75.

FOX, PHILIP S., "Observation with a Difference," *Journal of Health, Physical Education and Recreation,* XXXIII (January, 1962), pp. 40–42.

―――, "Participation: The Missing Link," *ibid.,* XXXIV (February, 1963), pp. 32, 75.

―――, "Student Teaching: The Culminating Experience," *ibid.,* XXXV (April, 1964), pp. 39–40, 88–89.

HANBY, KENNETH R., and DAVID E. BELKA, "Beginning Teacher Tips in Health and Physical Education," *The Physical Educator,* XXI (October, 1964), pp. 107–11.

HARPER, LeROY A. and ADELAIDE M. HUNTER, "Put Theory into Practice Now," *Journal of Health, Physical Education and Recreation,* XXXII (September, 1961), p. 73.

PETERSON, KAY H., "Student Teaching: The Capstone," *The Physical Educator,* XXI (March, 1964), pp. 32–34.

SPURGEON, JOHN H., "Student Teacher Placement," *Journal of Health, Physical Education and Recreation,* XXXIII, p. 66.

Roles Played by Personnel in Student Teaching

CHAPTER 2

Student teaching is a learning experience, the value of which depends upon several individuals. Since an increasing number of colleges and universities are sending student teachers off-campus for this experience, it is quite evident that, in addition to the student teacher, the supervising teacher, cooperating school administrator, and college supervisor have significant roles to play.

Although the primary responsibility must be the supervising teacher's, each of the others must recognize the value of the experience and give their full support to the program. Without the complete cooperation of these four individuals, this phase of the teacher's preparation would be adversely affected and a less-qualified teacher would enter the profession.

THE ROLE OF THE STUDENT TEACHER

There are four major phases of the student-teaching experience.

Observation gives the student teacher an opportunity to observe individual pupils and to become familiar with class procedures. It also exposes him to the methods and techniques used by the supervising teacher.

Induction gives the student teacher some experience in teaching without assuming full responsibility for teaching a class. He may be asked by the supervising teacher to assist in the instruction of individual pupils, the preparation of teaching aids, the demonstration of certain skills, and the evaluation of pupils.

Teaching gives the student teacher an opportunity to make use of his professional education, including skills, techniques, and methods of teaching. This phase of the student-teaching experience follows observation and induction. The starting time for full-time teaching varies with the student teacher, and the decision is made cooperatively by the supervising teacher and the student teacher.

Evaluation gives the student teacher an indication of his strengths and weaknesses. Appraisals should be made by the supervising teacher, college supervisor, student teacher, and pupils.

The following suggestions should help the student teacher to have a pleasant and beneficial experience:

- ☐ Begin student teaching with a desire to become a successful physical education teacher.
- ☐ Maintain a positive attitude toward teaching during your student-teaching experience.
- ☐ Plan your class activities carefully and well in advance.
- ☐ Develop the ability to cooperate with others.
- ☐ Keep records and reports current.
- ☐ Become familiar with the physical education and general educational policies of the school.
- ☐ Observe the teaching of others in both physical education and other areas.
- ☐ Be prompt for all assignments and meetings.
- ☐ Dress appropriately for the physical education activities to be taught.
- ☐ Make a pleasing personal appearance by dressing properly for the occasion.
- ☐ Accept responsibility for additional assignments to activities related to physical education.

**THE ROLE
OF THE SUPERVISING TEACHER**

The supervising teacher plays two roles when working with a student teacher: he is both a professional teacher of pupils and a teacher's educator. As a teacher, his primary, legal responsibility is to teach the pupils in his classes; as an educator, his responsibility is to provide an environment which will foster the student-teacher's growth.

There is a close relationship between the two roles that the supervising teacher plays, because his legal responsibility will affect the decisions he makes as a teacher's educator. In his role as an educator, he should provide for the growth of the student teacher by:

- ☐ Orienting the student teacher to the philosophy, policies, personnel, and facilities of the school.
- ☐ Acquainting him with the community, so that he will achieve a better understanding of the pupils in the classes.
- ☐ Arranging his induction so that he is gradually made ready for full-time teaching.
- ☐ Assisting him to understand the pupils.
- ☐ Assisting him to develop instructional skills in physical education.
- ☐ Familiarizing him with the audiovisual aids used in physical education.
- ☐ Assisting him in the preparation of teaching units, lesson plans, and techniques for evaluating the pupils.
- ☐ Guiding his professional growth.
- ☐ Helping him to develop the ability to evaluate and improve his own performance.

THE ROLE OF THE COLLEGE SUPERVISOR

The college supervisor is the liaison between his institution and the cooperating schools. It is also his responsibility to assist the student teacher's preparation in every possible way. It is hoped that he will develop a close, personal relationship with the student teacher.

He represents the college to the cooperating schools and is a key person in building good public relations. It is his responsibility to interpret the college's policy regarding student teaching to the cooperating school.

The role and responsibilities of the college supervisor have been stated as follows by the Association for Student Teaching:

1. Assist the director of student teaching in the assignment of student teachers and recommend reassignment when necessary.
2. Orient student teachers to the school environment in which they will do their student teaching.
3. Establish and maintain good relationships between colleges and cooperating schools.
4. Acquaint cooperating school personnel with the philosophy, objectives, organization, and content of the teacher education program.

5. Learn the philosophy, objectives, organization, and content of the cooperating school program.
6. Help supervising teachers and other members of the supervisory team understand and hence improve their performance in their supervisory role in the teacher education program.
7. Work with college and cooperating school personnel in planning an appropriate program of experiences for student teachers.
8. Observe and confer with student teachers in order to help them improve their instructional practices through clinical experiences in which the teaching-learning situation and related planning and evaluation activities are examined.
9. Consult with supervising teachers and other professionals in order to analyze the performance of student teachers and plan experiences that will lead to their greater understanding and, therefore, to the improvement of their teaching.
10. Counsel with student teachers concerning problems of adjustment to their teaching role.
11. Conduct seminars or teaching courses designated to supplement and complement student teaching experiences.
12. Consult with cooperating school personnel on curricular, instructional, and organizational matters when requested.
13. Analyze and refine their own professional skills.
14. Cooperate with other college and school personnel in evaluating and refining the teacher education program.[1]

THE ROLE OF THE COOPERATING-SCHOOL ADMINISTRATOR

The key person in the cooperating schools is the school administrator. He is a valuable member of the student-teaching team, and he should assume the following responsibilities:

- ☐ Recommend as supervising teachers members of his faculty who are qualified and willing.
- ☐ Assist in the assignment of student teachers, and coordinate the work of the student teacher and the cooperating physical education teacher.
- ☐ Help in the orientation of the student teacher by explaining the school's policies and procedures, through conferences and materials.

[1] Association for Student Teaching, *The College Supervisor* (Washington, D.C.: National Education Association, 1968), p. 13.

- ☐ Create a positive attitude toward student teaching among his staff and student body, and in the community.
- ☐ Accept the student teacher as a faculty member and give him every opportunity to understand the responsibilities of all teachers.
- ☐ Provide the supervising teacher with free time in which to conduct conferences with the student teacher.
- ☐ Arrange for the student teacher to observe teachers other than the assigned cooperating teacher.
- ☐ Encourage the student teacher to participate in the physical education extra-class activities, all school activities, and community functions.
- ☐ Keep the college supervisor informed about changes in teaching staff which might affect the student-teaching program.
- ☐ Work with the college supervisor toward the continuous improvement of the student-teaching experience in physical education.

part **II**

STUDENT TEACHING:

how, when?

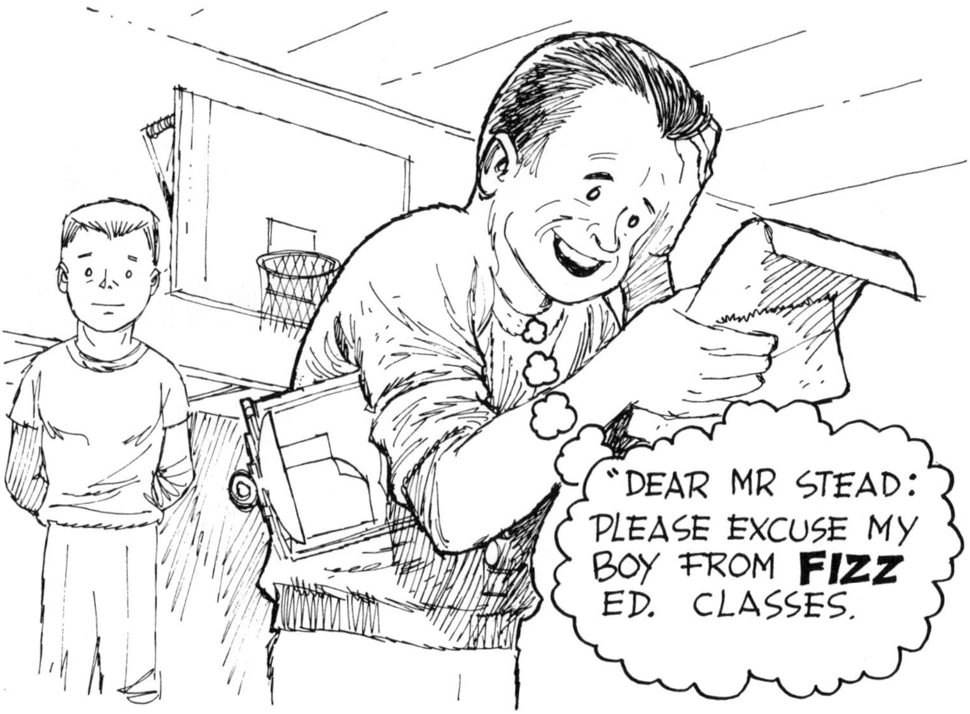
"DEAR MR STEAD: PLEASE EXCUSE MY BOY FROM **FIZZ** ED. CLASSES.

Elementary   CHAPTER 3

and

Secondary-School Class

and

Extra-Class Programs

**THE PHYSICAL EDUCATION
CLASS PROGRAM**

The program of physical education should be based on the needs of individual pupils and the communities where they live, and planned and conducted so that it contributes to the fulfillment of the purposes of education and the objectives of physical education.

**THE PHILOSOPHY
OF PHYSICAL EDUCATION**

One of the major needs of man has always been the need for movement. Physical activity is a constructive force, essential to the growth and development of all children and youth. Such elements as heredity, rest, sleep, diet, and many others affect the functioning of the whole person and, as such, are known as "conditioning" factors. These contributing factors form the basis upon which, through physical activity, such qualities as coordination, strength, balance, speed, and endurance can be developed. In order to insure youth an opportunity to be physically fit, it is necessary to make adequate provision for physical activities in their everyday living.

The biological urge for physical activity is nature's way of developing children and youth. The basic design for mankind has not changed: He is still meant to be the active, spirited organism that he has always been. However, the changes in civilization in the past few decades, and the coming of the age of automation, have made man less physically active than ever before in his history.

Without vigorous activities our children will develop neither physically nor mentally as they should. The human being cannot be divided into a mind and a body. All our physical, emotional, and social qualities are so interrelated that they are impossible to separate. Physical education, as a part of the total educational program, has as its purpose to develop the whole child so that he is able to become a physically, mentally, emotionally, and socially fit citizen.

THE OBJECTIVES OF PHYSICAL EDUCATION

Physical activities, carefully selected and conducted under desirable leadership, contribute to the development of the physical fitness and motor skills of each pupil, as well as of his knowledge and appreciation and social and democratic competence.

PHYSICAL FITNESS

Physical education's unique contribution to the total curriculum is the building of physical power in each pupil through the development of the body. Physical fitness is the ability of the individual to sustain adaptive effort, the ability to recover, and the ability to resist fatigue. Each pupil becomes more active, performs better, and is healthier if his body is adequately developed and functioning properly.

The physical education program must provide for the physical development of all children. No other area of the curriculum can meet this need. It is only through such natural activities as hanging, climbing, running, throwing, leaping, and jumping that adequate physical development is obtained. The end result of these activities is that each individual has the vitality, strength, and endurance for routine work or play. More, he is prepared for the requirements and emergencies of everyday living, which may vary from year to year, month to month, week to week, or day to day.

MOTOR SKILLS

"Motor skills' refer to the pupil's ability to perform physical movements with a minimum amount of energy and in a proficient and graceful manner. The program of physical education tries to develop in each pupil a variety of physical skills that he enjoys using and will enjoy in later life.

It takes several years for most people to acquire coordination, and the most important period for its development is during the formative years. Therefore, in order to attain skill, it is necessary to start teaching many activities early in life and continue the teaching into adulthood. Skills not acquired during youth are often never acquired. The physical education program should include the teaching of many skills when a person is young, and the teaching should progress throughout the school years. The acquisition of motor skills is important for the citizen of tomorrow. As a people we are constantly experiencing an increase in our leisure time. What we do with this leisure will determine to a great extent the quality of our civilization. One of the major tasks of the schools is to prepare youth to use their leisure well. The physical education program, by developing physical skills which may be enjoyed today and in the future, can make a major contribution.

KNOWLEDGE AND APPRECIATION OF PHYSICAL ACTIVITIES

Imparting a knowledge of physical activities and an appreciation of them should be an important aspect of the physical education program. All physical activities are learned; consequently, they involve thinking and result in the acquisition of knowledge. Besides the motor skills, every pupil should acquire a knowledge and appreciation of such things as rules, regulations, techniques, strategies, and the history of various physical activities. It is often easier to motivate pupils to seek knowledge through physical activities than through regular classroom assignments. You can teach number concepts in the third grade, for example, using the game of "Steal the Bacon," and you can teach something about Holland by having the pupils in the fifth grade participate in a Dutch dance.

The acquisition of knowledge about health is also an important part of the physical education program. Every pupil should know about such things as the importance of sanitation, factors in disease prevention, the importance of exercise, and the need for a well-balanced diet. This knowledge will contribute greatly to his general health and help him to live a more purposeful life. The power to think quickly, to interpret a situation correctly, to make an accurate judgment, and to act on it may be developed on the playground and in the gymnasium. Participation in physical education activities will help each pupil to make the discriminatory decisions by which a knowledge of values is derived.

SOCIAL COMPETENCE

Social competence involves the pupil's everyday adjustments to other individuals and to his group. It is of the utmost importance that every child become socially competent, able to take his place and play his part as a worthy member of the community. Activities in the physical education program are an excellent medium for the development of an understanding and appreciation of human nature. It is here that one of the best opportunities for making personal and group adjustment exists, if there is proper leadership. A pupil can learn to be a good sport only through experience, and no program offers more opportunities than physical education.

PROGRAM PLANNING

The program should be diversified so that it can offer the best possible opportunities for the growth and development of the pupils. This requires that there be many activities and that they be introduced at the appropriate grade and growth level.

For the sake of convenience, physical education class-instruction activities are grouped into the following categories:

Games. Includes team, individual, and dual.
Self-testing. Includes stunts, tumbling, and apparatus.
Dance. Includes basic rhythms, folk, square, modern, and social.
Body mechanics. Includes standing, walking, and running.
Aquatics. Includes swimming, diving, and water safety.
Remedial and adaptive.

Each school district should have a written course of study that will help give direction to program and provide for progression and continuity in class instruction throughout all grades. This guide should reflect the philosophy of the school administration and the physical education staff and their view of the place of physical education in the total curriculum. The planning and development of the guide should be primarily the work of the teachers and administrators. After it has been approved by the administration and board of education, the teachers should use it as a guide in the conduct of the program.

Each type of activity makes a certain contribution to the objectives of physical education. It is therefore necessary to offer all these types of activities. Each pupil should receive instruction not only in skills that he can use during his school years but in other skills, as well, that may be used during his lifetime.

The following general recommendations may be used as guidelines in planning the physical education program:

ELEMENTARY, SECONDARY-SCHOOL CLASS, EXTRA-CLASS PROGRAMS 25

- ☐ The program should be based on the interests and needs of every boy and girl.
- ☐ All pupils should participate in one or more parts of the physical education program daily.
- ☐ Boys and girls should have equal opportunities to participate in a variety of activities.
- ☐ Provision should be made for certain coeducational activities.
- ☐ Adequate time, staff, and facilities should be available for the program planned.
- ☐ Pupils and teachers should dress in a costume that is appropriate to the activities being taught and which permits safe participation in the activities.
- ☐ Showering, an integral part of the health and physical education program, should be required of all pupils who have participated in vigorous physical activity.
- ☐ The program should provide for instruction in the proper care of equipment, supplies, lockers, and contents, and in the proper use of toilet, dressing, and showering facilities.
- ☐ Pupils who are well enough to attend school should be considered well enough to attend physical education classes, but the teacher should adapt the activities to meet the individual pupil's needs, ranging from rest to limited participation.
- ☐ Elementary-grade pupils should not be denied opportunities for participating in the physical education program because they have misbehaved in the classroom.
- ☐ High-school pupils should not be excused from physical education classes because they are on a school team.
- ☐ Marks should not be used as a basis for determining eligibility for athletics.
- ☐ Such activities as dance lessons, band, R.O.T.C., and drill teams should not be accepted as substitutes for physical education.

PROGRAM ACTIVITIES

All pupils should have opportunities for instruction and practice in physical education activities through class instruction in regularly scheduled physical education classes, special-activity classes when necessary, and extra-class activities.

The physical education program consists of four basic parts:

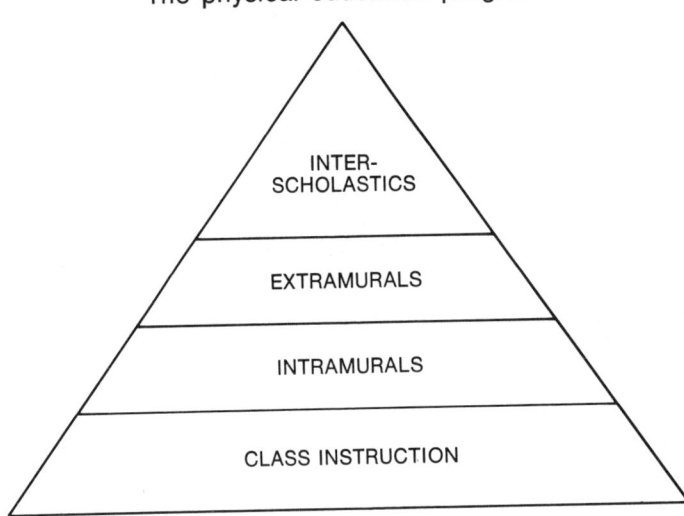

```
        /\
       /  \
      / INTER- \
     / SCHOLASTICS \
    /--------------\
   /  EXTRAMURALS   \
  /------------------\
 /    INTRAMURALS     \
/----------------------\
/   CLASS INSTRUCTION   \
--------------------------
```

CLASS INSTRUCTION

Class instruction is for all pupils, including members of the interscholastic teams. This is the broad base of the physical education program.

Pupils who need additional instruction or who are unable to participate profitably in the regular physical education class activities—a determination made through the health examination or by tests of physical fitness, posture, skill, and so on—should be offered classes adapted to their needs. Whenever possible, the students scheduled for these special classes should also participate in the regular classes, however. The special-activity classes should be planned and conducted with the approval of a physician—more specifically, a school physician if there is one in the school district.

The class-instruction part of the program should serve as the basis for extra-class activities, which should be considered physical education laboratory periods. Extra-class activities should be an outgrowth of the regularly scheduled classes.

THE EXTRA-CLASS PROGRAM

Extra-class activities are those which are conducted outside the regularly scheduled class-instruction periods. The purpose of such activities is to enrich the class instruction with additional instruction, practice, and competition. The administration and supervision of the extra-class program should be the responsibility of a physical educator, officially appointed and certified to teach or direct physical education.

Intramurals. Intramurals are those activities which are organized and conducted within one school and which include only those pupils enrolled in that school. The word "intramural" is derived from the Latin *intra*, meaning "within," and *muralis*, meaning "pertaining to a wall." These activities, a natural outgrowth of the class instruction, should be voluntary. They are basically for pupils of moderate ability who are not participating in interscholastic competition.

Extramurals. Extramurals are those activities—sports days, play days, or other approved interschool activities—which are conducted without a season-long schedule, league competition, or championship. On *sports days*, pupils from two or more schools participate in one or more activities but retain their school identity. On *play days*, pupils from two or more schools participate in one or more activities without retaining their school identity. This phase of the physical education program should also be voluntary. It is for pupils who want to play with and against pupils from other schools but who do not wish to play on a regularly scheduled interscholastic basis.

Interscholastics. Interscholastics are athletic activities which offer enriched opportunities for the more highly skilled pupils to represent a school in competition with pupils from other schools. These activities involve season-long schedules, organized practice, league competition, and championships, and are for pupils with above-average or exceptional athletic ability. This part of the physical education program is in line with the modern philosophy, which emphasizes the needs of the exceptional and talented student. Interscholastics require special facilities, special equipment, and special teachers to coach and supervise.

EXTRA-CLASS ACTIVITIES

For an extra-class program to be considered a good one, it must offer certain opportunities to pupils in all three phases of the extra-class program: intramurals; extramurals; and interscholastics.

Intramural activities. A good program of intramural activities will:

- ☐ Give all pupils an opportunity to choose from a variety of activities.
- ☐ Encourage the participation of all pupils, including those who do not perform well.
- ☐ Stress that the pleasure of participation is the main objective. There should be no excessive pressure to win.
- ☐ Allow the pupils to participate in the planning and organizing of the intramural activities.

28   STUDENT TEACHING: HOW, WHEN?

- ☐ Exclude pupils who participate in the same sport on an interscholastic team.
- ☐ Give careful consideration to scheduling the various activities so that pupils will receive prior instruction in the activity in the regular physical education classes. However, when this instruction is not possible—e.g., for skiing and horseback riding—the instruction should become an integral part of the intramural program. Although the main purpose of the intramural activities is to promote the pupils' participation, the teacher should be constantly alert to opportunities to teach additional skills and knowledge during the intramurals.
- ☐ Provide adequate time for the use of facilities, preferably after school or on Saturdays. When after-school schedules conflict, it will be necessary to schedule intramurals during the noon hour or activity period.
- ☐ Organize leagues and tournaments in such a manner that there will be equal competition. Frequently, schools will have a teacher select a captain for each team, and he, in turn, will select the players for his team. This is a good method of equating teams because pupils generally know the proficiency of their peers.
- ☐ Offer coeducational opportunities in such activities as archery, badminton, bowling, golf, skiing, swimming, table tennis, tennis, and volleyball.

Extramural activities.   A good program of extramural activities will:

- ☐ Offer a wide variety of activities to enrich the experiences of as many pupils as possible.
- ☐ Stimulate many pupils to participate in the intramural activities.
- ☐ Teach students to officiate and use them as officials during the games.
- ☐ Include the transportation and the use of facilities in the regular scheduling of extra-class activities for boys and girls.
- ☐ Never be used as a substitute or replacement for intramural activities.
- ☐ Exclude pupils who participate in the same sport on an interscholastic team.
- ☐ Offer coeducational opportunities in such activities as archery, badminton, bowling, golf, skiing, swimming, table tennis, tennis, and volleyball.

Interscholastic activities.   A good program of interscholastic activities will:

- ☐ Be an effectively organized and well-coordinated phase of the secondary-school curriculum, and an integrated and balanced part of the total physical education program.

- ☐ Receive a share of tax funds and school facilities, since it is an integral part of the education program.
- ☐ Promote amateurism, rather than professionalism and commercialism.
- ☐ Include a wide variety of activities during each sports season, so that all pupils may participate.
- ☐ Promote ethics and sportsmanship among the participants, spectators, and coaches.
- ☐ Teach respect for the rules and regulations of games, and emphasize health and safety.
- ☐ Help to form leagues which sponsor all sports of interest to schools of similar size in the same geographic location. The function of the league is to organize, plan, promote, and administer activities in an educationally sound manner.
- ☐ Cover all participants with adequate and appropriate insurance, in case of injury.
- ☐ Not establish scholastic eligibility standards for interschool competition. It is not sound, educationally, to permit the use of standards in one part of the curriculum to determine whether a pupil may participate in another part of the curriculum.
- ☐ Restrict pupils on an interscholastic team by not allowing them to play the same sport on an intramural or extramural basis.
- ☐ Not be used as a substitute for class instruction in physical education. All pupils who are on interscholastic teams should still attend physical education classes.

class program: situations and analysis

**FIRST SITUATION:
DISCIPLINE BY ANOTHER TEACHER**

In her first teaching assignment at Broadway Elementary School, Miss Means finds that one of the classes reporting for physical education lacks several pupils. After conferring with their classroom teacher, Miss Means finds that she kept the children in the classroom as a disciplinary measure because they misbehaved.

QUESTIONS

Should an elementary-school classroom teacher be able to keep pupils in the classroom as a disciplinary measure while other pupils in the same class are participating in scheduled physical education? What would be acceptable disciplinary measures for the classroom teacher to take? Should there be an administrative policy which determines how teachers should discipline pupils?

ANALYSIS

It is not educationally sound for a classroom teacher to keep a pupil out of scheduled physical education. The elementary-grade pupil has great need for vigorous activity. At this age level, it is essential that all pupils receive instruction in the basic skills related to physical education. Disciplinary measures will vary with the type and extent of misbehavior of the pupil, but in no case should a pupil be removed from the physical-education program as a disciplinary measure.

In order to make sure that all pupils are treated fairly and that individual teachers have guidance about disciplinary procedures, administrative policies should be established and made known to all teachers. Miss Means should check with the principal of the school to see if there are any such policies.

SECOND SITUATION
THE BALLET DANCER

Miss Jones, the girls' physical education teacher at Ontario High School, has received a telephone call from a mother who wants her daughter excused from physical education because she is taking ballet lessons. The mother thinks that her daughter is getting enough exercise and could better spend her time in study hall.

QUESTIONS

Does ballet make a contribution to a girl's body development? Is body development the only objective of the physical education program? Can the total objectives of physical education be met through ballet lessons?

ANALYSIS

Ballet has definite value in the development of the total body. However, its primary contribution is to the development of the lower extremities. In order to develop the total body, it is necessary for pupils to participate in a variety of physical education activities—games, gymnastics, and swimming.

Body development makes a contribution to physical fitness and is the unique objective of physical education. However, there are other important objectives of the program, such as skills, knowledges, and social competence. Ballet contributes to the development of skills, knowledge, and social competence, but only in relation to this specific activity. It makes little or no contribution to these objectives as they are related to the many activities that should be included in a good program of physical education.

Miss Jones, in her conversation with the mother, should indicate the desirability of ballet lessons. Her daughter's interest and skill in ballet will make her of great assistance to Miss Jones as a leader and demonstrator of rhythms and dance activities. It should also be mentioned to the parent that ballet dancing, for most people, does not have great carry-over value and that there are numerous other activities which pupils participate in which they will engage in in later life.

THIRD SITUATION: SHOWERING

Mr. Scott, the new Director of Physical Education for the Jamestown Public Schools, is alarmed to find that most pupils in the schools do not take showers after participating in physical activity. The high school physical education teachers complain that a 45 minute period is not long enough for the pupils to shower. The elementary schools have dressing-showering facilities but do not use the showers.

QUESTIONS

Why should pupils take showers? Is a 45-minute period enough time to include showering? At what grade level should showering be initiated? Should there be an administrative policy in regard to showering?

ANALYSIS

Showering is recognized as an integral part of the health and physical education programs. If the programs of health teaching and health guidance are to be effective, and if personal health standards are to be maintained by individual pupils, the taking of a shower after physical activity is essential.

It should be the responsibility of the school to facilitate this phase of the program by proper scheduling. This is especially true in the elementary grades, where many of the physical education classes are scheduled for 25 to 30 minutes. This is not sufficient time for class activities plus dressing and showering. It is recommended that these periods be extended to 45 minutes so that pupils have adequate time to dress and shower properly.

Many schools have their pupils shower by the third or fourth grade. When schools initiate showering in these grades, there are usually fewer problems about it in the junior and senior high-school grades. Eight to twelve-year-old pupils are ready for showering and should not be denied the opportunity of establishing this desirable health practice. With these youngsters, the problem is not getting them into the shower, but getting them out of the shower.

There should be an administrative policy in regard to showering. This policy should be thoroughly discussed with the pupils by the physical education teachers so that it is understood by the pupils. In some school districts, it is a matter of educating not only the pupils but some of the parents as well.

FOURTH SITUATION:
DRESSING IN PHYSICAL EDUCATION UNIFORM

This is the first year that the boys in Belfast Junior High School have worn physical education uniforms. The pupils have been told to take their uniforms home every Friday to be laundered. On Monday, several pupils in each class have forgotten their uniforms. What can the teacher, Mr. Jones, do to alleviate the situation?

QUESTIONS

Is it desirable to have pupils dress in a uniform when participating in physical education activities? At what grade level should pupils begin wearing uniforms? Should pupils be required to take their uniforms home to be laundered every week? What procedures can be used to alleviate the situation when pupils forget their uniforms?

ANALYSIS

It is desirable to have pupils dress in a uniform because it will permit them to participate in the many activities with greater safety. A uniform contributes to the general appearance of the class and promotes *esprit de corps.*

In many schools, pupils start dressing in physical education uniforms in the third or fourth grade, and some schools require it even earlier. When the wearing of uniforms has been required in the elementary grades, there are usually fewer problems about dress in the high-school grades.

It is a desirable health practice to have clean clothing, and pupils should have their uniforms laundered each week. Many schools that have their own laundries make provision for cleaning physical education uniforms, but if the school does not have a laundry, the pupil should be required to take his uniform home.

There usually are a few pupils who forget their uniforms. To meet this emergency, Mr. Jones should have available a few uniforms of assorted sizes to lend to these pupils.

FIFTH SITUATION: AN UNCOORDINATED PROGRAM

There have been many problems in the physical education program in the Dalton Public Schools. There is no direction to the program and what takes place in each school depends pretty much on its principal. The superintendent of schools has asked the physical education staff for suggestions for improving the situation.

QUESTIONS

Why is it important to have direction to the physical education program? What steps can be taken to help establish direction to the program? Who should see that there is direction to the program?

ANALYSIS

It is important to have direction to the program established in order to be certain that all pupils receive instruction in all aspects of the program. Since physical education should be taught at all grade levels, it is imperative to have all pupils participate in a continuous, coordinated program.

A course of study should be developed by the physical education staff and submitted to the administration and board of education. To see that this course of study is properly implemented, a director or supervisor of physical education should be employed. This person, who has the technical knowledge, should serve in an advisory capacity to the principal and work cooperatively with him.

SIXTH SITUATION: THE NATIONAL GUARD

Mr. Bennett, a high school physical education teacher, received a note from Mrs. Jones, who wants her boy excused from physical education because he is in the National Guard. What should be Mr. Bennett's reaction to this request?

QUESTIONS

Does participation in the National Guard contribute to the objectives of physical education? Are there laws requiring pupils to take physical education classes?

ANALYSIS

Participation in the National Guard does make a limited contribution to the objectives of physical education, but its major emphasis is on military drill. This cannot possibly replace the varied offerings of a good physical education program, which stresses physical, mental, emotional, and social development through many different types of physical activities.

A majority of the states have laws which require that physical education be taught in the public schools, legislation which was usually initiated because the public was concerned about the lack of physical fitness of men going into the armed forces. Many military leaders have gone on record as indicating that drill is improved when the men have had physical education and that the greatest contribution the school can make is to make their students physically fit by means of a good physical education program.

DISCUSSION NOTES

**PERSONAL PRACTICE-TEACHING EXPERIENCE
RELATED TO THE TOPIC**

extra-class program: situations and analysis

FIRST SITUATION:
BOXING

A former collegiate boxer has just become the new high-school principal in Dansville. He is interested in starting a boxing team. The superintendent of schools has asked Mr. Merritt, the physical education teacher, to meet with him and the new principal to discuss the idea. What factors pertinent to this problem should be related by Mr. Merritt?

QUESTIONS

Should boxing be included as part of the physical education program? What are the harmful effects of boxing? What is a more desirable contact sport for boys?

ANALYSIS

Boxing should not be included as part of the physical education program because the objectives of boxing are not consonant with the objectives of physical education. No other activity in physical education has the objective of "putting away" the opposition.

The detrimental effect of cumulative blows on the head of a boxer makes boxing a definite hazard to the participant. Even headgear or a helmet does not prevent knockouts which damage the brain. Some exponents of the sport say that heavy gloves will prevent serious injuries, but there is a record of a death when 14-ounce gloves were used.

A more desirable contact sport for boys is wrestling, which is based on the principles of leverage as they apply to movement. The objectives of wrestling are consistent with the goals of physical education, since the intent of a wrestler is not to maim or cripple the opponent but to score more points.

SECOND SITUATION:
SCHOLASTIC ELIGIBILITY

Mr. Lewis, the high-school principal in Jeffersonville, would like to have scholastic-eligibility rules for the boys' interscholastic athletic competition. The physical education staff is not in favor of such a policy.

The superintendent of schools has indicated that no decision will be made until he and the board of education have heard both sides.

QUESTIONS

What eligibility standards do schools use? Are these eligibility policies consistent throughout the education curriculum? Are scholastic-eligibility standards for interscholastic athletic competition educationally sound?

ANALYSIS

Schools that use scholastic marks for determining a pupil's eligibility for playing on interscholastic teams usually have a set standard and determine eligibility on a weekly basis. In some schools the standard varies for each pupil, the teachers determining what they think each pupil is capable of attaining.

In many schools there are no consistent standards of eligibility. For example, a football player who is failing a subject may be prohibited from playing in the game on Saturday afternoon, but a band member who is failing the same subject may be allowed to march in the band at the same game. If a school has a policy of scholastic eligibility for extra-class activities, then this policy should apply to all activities, including plays, concerts, bands, and clubs.

Scholastic-eligibility standards for interschool competition are not educationally sound because they entail the use of standards in one part of the curriculum to determine whether a pupil may participate in another part of the curriculum. If interscholastic athletics are educational and a part of the physical education program, then it would make just as much sense to take a boy out of English because he is failing physical education. Often, when a pupil is not allowed to participate in interscholastic sports, the school is eliminating the one part of the curriculum that is of special interest to him. Invariably, the pupil will seek recognition in ways that are not desirable. There are certain things, such as teamwork and cooperation, that can best be taught in a sports program. This part of the educational curriculum should not be denied any pupil.

**THIRD SITUATION:
THE FOOTBALL PLAYER**

Mr. Evans, the football coach at Highland Falls High School, wants his football players excused from physical education because they get enough exercise. Mr. Tupper, the high-school principal, said he would permit this if it were all right with the physical-education department. Should the physical education department agree?

QUESTIONS

Why should a football player take physical education classes in the fall? Will a football player who also has physical education classes be involved in too much physical activity? Should a pupil playing on the football, basketball, and baseball team be excused from physical education?

ANALYSIS

A football player should take physical-education classes in the fall because the activities taught in physical education classes during the fall include more than football. There are skills in many other activities that he will not learn if he is excused from physical education.

The physical education teacher knows the pupils who are playing interscholastic sports and should make adjustments in their physical education class program. For example, when teaching a unit on punting, he could use the football players as demonstrators, and so limit their activity.

If pupils are to be truly physically educated, they should be exposed to and have the experience of participating in a variety of different physical education activities. They should become involved not only in team games, but also in individual and dual activities, self-testing activities, and aquatics. If excused from participating in physical education during a sports season, a pupil could graduate from high school without ever having been exposed to and possibly developing an interest in such activities as badminton, volleyball, wrestling, gymnastics, or swimming. The three-sport athlete, excused from physical education each sports season, would graduate with considerable proficiency in the three sports, but with little or no skill in any other physical education activity. As he becomes older, he will no longer be able to participate in football, basketball, and baseball and, unfortunately, he will have no background in the carry-over activities that he could engage in even when he is quite elderly.

FOURTH SITUATION:
UNEQUAL INTRAMURAL TEAMS

At Southside Junior High School, Mrs. Wilcox, the physical education teacher, finds that there are very few girls who have indicated a desire to participate in intramural activities. She has checked with the girls and finds that the lack of interest is due primarily to unequal competition among teams in the intramural league. What steps should Mrs. Wilcox take?

QUESTIONS

Should the teacher, or the pupils, select the intramural teams? How can intramural competition be equated? Should intramural teams be chosen for a specific sport season, or should the teams vary during each intramural period?

ANALYSIS

There appears to be a certain value in having pupils select their own intramural teams. A procedure used by many schools is for the teacher to select a captain for each team; he, in turn, selects the players. The players feel that they belong to a team because they have been chosen by another pupil, who is the captain. This seems to be the best procedure for equating teams because pupils generally know the proficiency of their peers. The problem at Southside Junior High School may have resulted because the teacher selected the teams, creating unequal competition, and creating the feeling among the players of belonging to a specific team because they were assigned by the teacher rather than being chosen.

Most pupils participating in intramural activities would prefer to be identified with a specific team during a particular sport season. This gives the student a sense of belonging to a particular unit, and his place on the team becomes of considerable importance to him and his teammates.

FIFTH SITUATION: LIMITING TEAM MEMBERSHIP

In Carlisle High School, Mr. Whiting, the new principal, is concerned with the interscholastic program. He finds that there is no limit to the number of different athletic teams on which a pupil may participate during a given sports season. What action should Mr. Whiting take?

QUESTIONS

Should a pupil be allowed to participate on more than one interscholastic team during a sports season? Should a pupil who participates on an interschool team be permitted to play on an intramural team? Should an athlete be allowed to participate on a varsity and a junior varsity team in the same sport?

ANALYSIS

It is undesirable for a pupil to participate on more than one interscholastic team during a particular sports season because of the adverse effects upon his health. In schools where there is not adequate enrollment to have a great many athletic teams, the number of interscholastic sports should be limited.

A pupil who participates on an interschool team should not be permitted to participate on an intramural team in the same sport. The interscholastics are for the above-average and highly skilled pupils. The purpose of the intramural phase of the program is to provide opportunities for pupils of moderate ability to participate in many activities. Schools that permit their interscholastic team members to participate in the intramural program in the same sport deprive other pupils of opportunities. However, it is generally agreed that it is desirable to allow pupils on an interscholastic team to participate on an intramural basis in a different sport.

In most situations, an athlete should not be allowed to participate on a varsity and junior varsity team at the same time. Schools that permit him to do so limit the number of different pupils who may participate in an activity and create situations of unequal competition. When there is limited enrollment it would be advisable to have the school represented by just one team.

Mr. Whiting should work cooperatively with the physical education and coaching staff in the development of policies to be adhered to by coaches in all sports. These policies should be based upon the best interests of the pupils as indicated in the above statements.

DISCUSSION NOTES

**PERSONAL PRACTICE-TEACHING EXPERIENCE
RELATED TO TOPIC**

SELECTED REFERENCES

BUCHER, CHARLES A., *Administration of School and College Health and Physical Education Programs.* St. Louis: The C. V. Mosby Company, 1967.

————, *Foundations of Physical Education.* St. Louis: The C. V. Mosby Company, 1964.

COWELL, C. C., and H. W. HAZELTON, *Curriculum Designs in Physical Education.* Englewood Cliffs, N.J.: Prentice-Hall, Inc., 1951.

GEORGE, JACK F., and HARRY A. LEHMANN, *School Athletic Administration.* New York: Harper & Row, Publishers, Incorporated, 1966.

NIXON, JOHN E., and ANN E. JEWETT, *Physical Education Curriculum.* New York: The Ronald Press Company, 1964.

VOLTMER, EDWARD F., and ARTHUR A. ESSLINGER, *The Organization* and *Administration of Physical Education.* New York: Appleton-Century-Crofts, 1966.

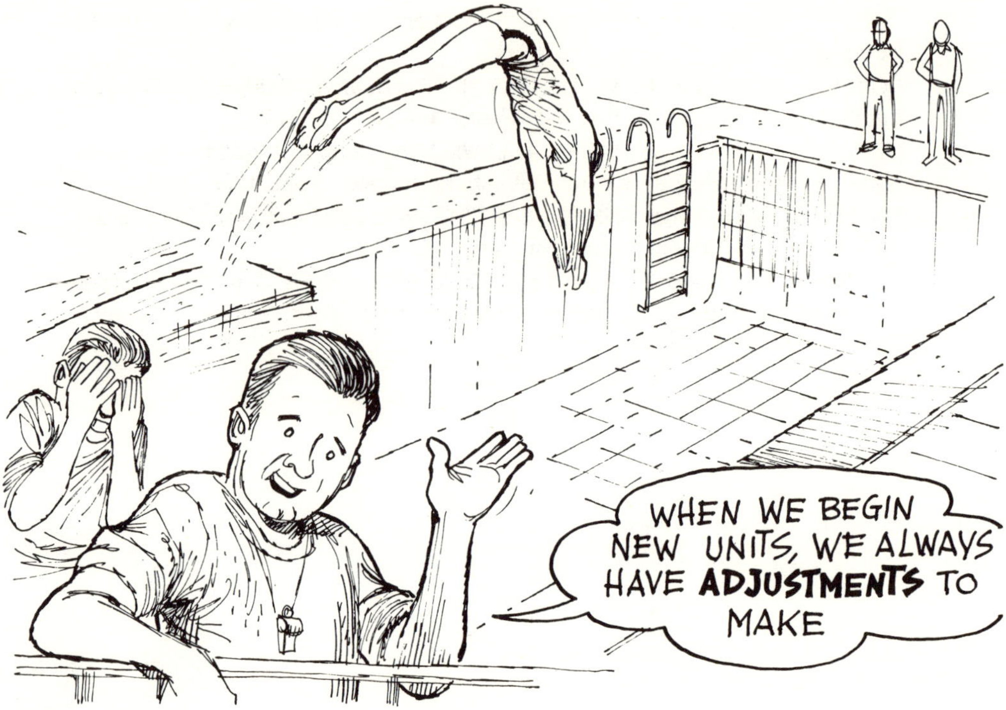
WHEN WE BEGIN NEW UNITS, WE ALWAYS HAVE **ADJUSTMENTS** TO MAKE

Swimming CHAPTER 4
Pools

Swimming is one of the most beneficial of all physical education activities. Swimming offers great physiological, psychological, social, and recreational benefits, and of course contributes to safety. These factors, plus the increased popularity of swimming among children, youth and adults, place a responsibility on schools to teach aquatic activities and water safety.

School swimming pools are worthwhile educational facilities which contribute to the development of children, better prepare them to take their place in society, and enrich their lives.

CONTRIBUTIONS OF SWIMMING AND WATER SAFETY

One of the primary objectives of education is the development of physical and mental health. Training in swimming and water safety contributes to this objective in the following ways:

☐ Physical fitness. Swimming is one of the best all-around types of physical activity. It contributes to the development and maintenance of strength, cardiovascular efficiency, and neuromuscular coordination.

☐ Therapeutic value. Swimming is an effective means for helping individuals with physical handicaps and mental disorders. The buoyancy of water permits handicapped persons to perform activities that they may have difficulty performing out of water. It can offer these people opportunities to acquire skills and achieve levels of success that ordinarily would not be possible. The blind, the amputee, the paralyzed, the spastic, and the injured have, through swimming, an outlet for physical expression that is not available in most other activities.

☐ Safety. Drowning is the fourth-ranking cause of accidental deaths. Approximately 47 per cent of those drowned each year are children of school age. Accidents can be prevented, and one of the best ways is to teach people how and where to swim. Instruction in swimming, water safety, and lifesaving can reduce accidents.

☐ Recreation. Swimming is one of the most enjoyable recreational activities, particularly for children. It possesses a great deal of carry-over value into adult life. Participation can be on an individual, coeducational, family, and community basis, and at any age.

☐ Social values. Swimming offers numerous chances to develop such worthwhile social attributes as self-confidence, cooperation, respect for others, observing rules, and respect for authority.

☐ Vocational preparation. Swimming may lead to such vocational opportunities as lifeguard, swimming and water-safety instructor, recreation leader, or physical education teacher. It may also be of value in occupations such as commercial fishing and ship transportation.

☐ Juvenile delinquency. Although swimming pools in themselves do not prevent juvenile delinquency, they can contribute in a positive way toward the reduction of delinquency.

PUBLIC INTEREST AND SUPPORT FOR A SWIMMING POOL

Obtaining public interest and support is an essential part of the planning for a school swimming pool. Some general procedures include:

☐ Organize a planning group. This group should represent all community interests and demonstrate the need for a swimming pool.
☐ Identify those individuals and groups that oppose the swimming pool and neutralize or win them over. People who have the respect and goodwill of the objectors should speak with them individually or in small groups.
☐ Obtain the advice of aquatic specialists so that all technical information is correct.
☐ Clarify the high cost in terms of numbers using the pool, hours of use, and difference in cost of another physical education teaching station.
☐ Sell the idea and value of a swimming pool before its cost and financing are figured out.

THE SCHOOL SWIMMING PROGRAM

A school swimming and water-safety program must be based on the needs and interests of students and the goals to be achieved. Factors that should be considered include: (1) facilities; (2) age, grade, and competence of students; (3) instructional periods scheduled per week; and (4) community interest and participation in water activities.

The goals of a school swimming program include:

- ☐ Teaching students to develop skill and understanding, so they can become competent and safe swimmers.
- ☐ Teaching students the basics of water safety, and assisting those who possess the ability to obtain lifesaving certificates.
- ☐ Providing opportunity for a comprehensive program of extra-class instruction that includes advanced swimming and a variety of aquatic activities.
- ☐ Permitting children, youth, and adults the opportunity to take part in swimming and water-safety activities during the evening, on weekends, and in the summer.
- ☐ Developing lifelong attitudes concerning safe and satisfying participation in aquatic activities.

THE ADMINISTRATION OF A SCHOOL AQUATICS PROGRAM

The administration of a school aquatics program involves a number of major factors. Some of these include responsibility, instructional staff, program development, program, policies and procedures, and scheduling.

All programs conducted by school districts are under the jurisdiction of the board of education. However, the chief school officer administers these programs and delegates specific responsibilities to members of his staff. Since swimming and water safety are part of the physical education curriculum, the director of physical education and his staff assume this responsibility. Those responsible for the aquatics program should be certified physical education teachers. They should possess water-safety instructors' certificates, which signifies competence in aquatic-safety skills and teaching methods.

There should be an over-all plan for a year-round swimming and water-safety program. Through such a plan, desired goals may be achieved and existing staff and facilities can be used to their maximum. The plan should be part of the school district's physical education and recreation programs. Efforts should also be made to cooperate with municipal recreation and parks departments, as well as with volunteer youth agencies, in order to develop a community aquatics program. The program should be comprehensive, open to people of different ages, and include many activities. The fundamentals of swimming and water safety should be taught to all pupils who have not qualified as swimmers. Advanced instruction in aquatics should be provided for those who possess the ability. Numerous opportunities should be available for everyone to participate in aquatics through intramural, interscholastic, and recreational activities.

Policies and procedures concerning the use of the swimming pool should be established cooperatively by the director of physical education and his staff. All policies and rules should be approved by the board of education and posted where they may be read, and they should cover such matters as:

- ☐ Physical examination.
- ☐ Organic defects.
- ☐ Excuses.
- ☐ Supervision.
- ☐ First aid.
- ☐ Swimming suits, towels, and bathing caps.
- ☐ Behavior in the pool and pool area.
- ☐ Equipment.
- ☐ Locker rooms.
- ☐ Entering the pool.
- ☐ Leaving the pool.

Since school aquatic facilities are usually too limited to meet everyone's needs, it is necessary to schedule their use during the school day, after school, on weekends, in the evening, and in the summer. In districts where one pool may serve a number of elementary schools, one or more junior-high schools, and a senior-high school, the scheduling problem is more intricate. Priority should be given to those pupils who have not yet learned how to swim. The situation can be alleviated by using "instructional type" pools in the elementary schools, or portable pools which may be moved to different schools or areas of the community.

THE DESIGN AND CONSTRUCTION OF SWIMMING POOLS

The design, construction, and operation of a swimming pool should be based upon the needs and interests of the school and community

SWIMMING POOLS 49

that it serves. The pool should be considered an essential teaching station for physical education and, therefore, should be included in the plans of a new school building, rather than being an addition. This is of the utmost importance when school bond issues are being presented to the voters.

A number of guidelines should be kept in mind when designing and constructing swimming pools. These include:

- ☐ Location. The pool should be close to the other physical education facilities, but its entrances and exits should be planned with the community in mind.
- ☐ Shape and size. The most common shape for instructional pools is rectangular. Modifications of this type of pool are the L and T designs, the base of the L and the top of the T being used for diving. A pool to be used for competition should be 75 feet and 1 inch long.
- ☐ Construction. Different types of materials are available for pool construction: poured concrete, steel, brick, cement block, plastic or vinyl, and aluminum. Poured and reinforced concrete has been used successfully in many school swimming pools.
- ☐ Surface. A number of finishes are used for swimming pools, including tile, marble dust, paint, natural concrete, glazed brick, and plaster. Although most expensive, tile is permanent and is considered by many to be the best.
- ☐ Deck area. There should be sufficient space around the pool for demonstration, practice drills, and relaxation. The deck area should be 6 to 10 feet wide at the shallow end and at the sides of the pool, and 15 to 20 feet wide at the deep end.
- ☐ Pool markings. Markings should be permanently imbedded in the building material. Depth markings should be placed at intervals along the top deck on each side of the pool. Lane lines should be marked, the number to be determined by the width of the pool.
- ☐ Diving boards. Diving boards are made of wood, fiberglass, and aluminum. Indoor diving boards are 1 and 3 meters. Their height and number will usually be determined by the depth of the water, the height of the ceiling, and the size of the pool.
- ☐ Lighting. Adequate lighting is extremely important. Natural lighting without glare can be obtained with blister and glass-brick types of skylights. Artificial lighting should have recessed fixtures. Consideration should be given, in the design of the lighting system, to servicing the fixtures in the ceiling over the water. At water level, there should be a minimum of 20 foot-candles of illumination.
- ☐ Heating and ventilating. The air temperature should be 5° to 7° F. warmer than the water temperature. Forced ventilation is required to reduce humidity and condensation.

☐ Acoustical treatment. The ceiling and walls should be treated with waterproof acoustical material in order to reduce noise and permit the teacher to carry on class instruction.

☐ Storage space. There should be a storage room for instructional and cleaning equipment in the pool area.

☐ Office. A swimming-pool office should have windows facing the pool, and so situated that one can see the entire pool. The office should contain a telephone.

☐ Spectator space. This area should permit the entire pool to be visible without obstruction, yet be separated sufficiently from the pool. Seating may be either permanent, semipermanent or roll-away, or temporary.

☐ Safety equipment. Safety equipment such as buoys with throwing lines, rescue poles, first-aid kit, and an emergency telephone with an outside line should be provided.

swimming situations and analysis

**FIRST SITUATION:
PROMOTING A SCHOOL SWIMMING POOL**

The board of education has asked the physical education staff in the Garden City Public Schools to give them information to be used in the promotion of a swimming pool in the new building program at the senior high school. The information will be used at various citizens' meetings throughout the school district.

QUESTIONS

Should swimming be included as part of the physical education program? What values are derived from participation in swimming? What factors affect the cost of a pool?

ANALYSIS

Swimming is one of the most valuable activities in the physical education program. It contributes to the physiological development, psychological satisfaction, social adjustment, recreation, and safety skills of the individual.

Two important facts that should be considered when discussing the importance of swimming pools are: (1) nearly two out of three people in the United States cannot swim well enough to pass a simple swimming test of 50 feet; (2) approximately 6,800 people lose their lives yearly in the United States through some type of water accident.

However, there are other important benefits besides safety to be gained from swimming:

- ☐ *Physical fitness.* Studies of competitive swimmers show that their physical fitness exceeds that of athletes in other sports.
- ☐ *Recreation.* Swimming is a very popular activity at all age levels, and thus is an excellent family recreation.
- ☐ *Safety.* School children account for approximately 47 per cent of the drownings annually. In addition to teaching swimming, the school also should teach all aspects of water safety.
- ☐ *Social competence.* Swimming contributes to the development of such desirable traits as self-reliance, confidence, and respect for rules and regulations.
- ☐ *Handicapped persons.* People who are handicapped, including the blind, deaf, and crippled, find swimming an enjoyable physical activity. The buoyancy of the water allows the handicapped person to make certain movements that he may not be able to make on land.

Some of the factors that affect the *cost of the pool* are size, materials used, cost of labor, special added features, number of windows, and the prior existence of certain facilities, such as dressing rooms and showers. Although the initial expense of a swimming pool may appear quite high, the annual cost over a period of time is quite reasonable, especially because the pool will be the most frequently used part of the school's facilities.

SECOND SITUATION: FINANCING THE SCHOOL SWIMMING POOL

The superintendent of schools in Canton has informed the physical education staff that the board of education would like to include a swimming pool in the new senior-high school being planned. They are undecided whether to include the pool in the regular building bond issue that is submitted to the voters for approval or submit it as a separate bond issue. They would like the recommendation of the physical education teachers.

QUESTIONS

Should a swimming pool be presented as part of a total building program? Is it easier to get the voters' approval of a swimming pool when it is part of a total building program? Is there danger of losing an entire building program by making the swimming pool part of it?

ANALYSIS

The question of whether a swimming pool should be constructed is a decision of the board of education and the voters of a community. Since swimming is an integral part of the physical education program, the swimming pool should be included in the total building program, as part of the physical education facilities.

Generally speaking, it is easier to get approval for swimming pools when they are made part of the total building program. Some surveys show that most existing swimming pools in schools were part of the total building program. A school district that has its residents vote on a swimming pool as a separate issue is, in essence, saying that swimming is not an integral part of the total educational program.

Contrary to the opinion of many people, a swimming pool can be a significant factor in winning approval for an entire building program. Some school administrators have stated that many voters have indicated to them that they voted for a new building program because it did include a swimming pool.

THIRD SITUATION:
LONG HAIR

Mr. Gray has several boys in swimming classes who have long hair. He believes this to be a health problem in the pool. Swimming is part of the required physical education program, and all boys must participate.

QUESTIONS

Does long hair create an unsanitary situation in the swimming pool? What should be done to eliminate this problem? What other conditions can create unsanitary situations in swimming pools? What steps should be taken to alleviate those situations?

ANALYSIS

Exposing long hair to the water in a swimming pool creates an unsanitary situation because the dirt, oil, and lint in the loose or fallen hairs clog the filters. Therefore, all swimmers with long hair should be required to wear a bathing cap.

Other conditions, such as athlete's foot, plantar warts, and skin lesions can also create unsanitary situations in swimming pools. All teachers of swimming should check pupils for these conditions before they enter the pool. Also, all pupils should be taught to report any organic defects to the teacher prior to entering the pool. It should be mandatory for all pupils to receive a complete health examination by a physician prior to attending swimming classes. The above steps should be stated in policy form and followed by all appropriate personnel.

FOURTH SITUATION: THE LOCATION OF THE POOL

The superintendent of schools has asked Mr. Bowdoin, the director of physical education, whether the swimming pool in the new building program should be located in the new elementary school or the new senior-high school. The elementary-school principal would like to have the facility in his school, and the high-school principal would like to have it in his building.

QUESTIONS

What are the benefits of having the swimming pool in the elementary school? What are the benefits of having the swimming pool in the secondary school? What adjustments should be made if the swimming pool is located in the elementary school? What adjustments should be made if the swimming pool is located in the secondary school?

ANALYSIS

Since statistics indicate that the 5-to-14 age group has a high frequency of deaths by drowning, it is apparent that elementary-school children should be taught swimming and water safety. If the swimming pool is located in the elementary school, it is much easier to schedule their lessons.

The main value of a swimming pool in a secondary school is related to its size and shape. Swimming pools in secondary schools are generally larger and deeper, permitting greater participation of youth and adults in the recreational swimming program. The greater depth of the high-school pool permits the teaching of additional aquatic activities, such as diving and lifesaving.

If there is no swimming pool in the high school and the pool is located in the elementary school, then it should be planned to accommodate all pupils and adults. In such cases, the slope of the bottom of the pool is important. Approximately 60 per cent of the pool area should be shallow water, for elementary-grade pupils, and 40 per cent of the pool area should be deeper water, so that youth and adults can engage in such activities as lifesaving, synchronized swimming, and diving.

If there is no swimming pool in the elementary school and the pool is located in the high school, then it should be planned to be used by elementary-grade pupils. Sixty percent of the pool area still should be shallow water, for teaching these pupils.

In school districts where there is a single swimming pool to serve several elementary schools, one or more junior-high schools, and a senior-high school, the problem of scheduling is complex. However, it is possible, by careful scheduling, to arrange for every pupil in the school district to participate in the swimming program.

FIFTH SITUATION:
ATHLETE'S FOOT

When Mrs. Brownell, the high-school physical education teacher, inspects the feet of the girls in her swimming classes, she finds many cases of athlete's foot. She is puzzled because there is a foot bath between the dressing room and the showering room, and every girl must step in this bath when leaving the showering room.

QUESTIONS

Is it good hygienic practice to have a foot bath at the entrance of the shower room? What practices should be taught to pupils to insure good foot hygiene? What other school personnel should Mrs. Brownell work with to solve this problem?

ANALYSIS

A foot bath at the entrance of the shower room is not recommended. Its value is negligible, and it soon becomes dirty, unsanitary, and unattractive. Foot baths are considered a hazard by some, because they tend to promote a false sense of security and lessen emphasis on the personal care of the feet.

General preventive practices should be taught to all pupils to insure good foot hygiene. The proper care of the feet should be stressed, including the wearing of clean and properly laundered socks, keeping shoes in a sanitary condition, wearing one's own socks and shoes, bathing the feet frequently, drying well between the toes, and using plain talcum powder with a 10-percent boric acid solution.

Since this is a health problem, all school personnel directly concerned with the teaching of health should work cooperatively with Mrs. Brownell. Such staff members as the school physician, school nurse, health education teacher, and director of physical education should be concerned with the problem.

SIXTH SITUATION: EXCUSING GIRL SWIMMERS

Pupils at Haywood High School participate in swimming classes one day a week. This year the twelfth-grade boys attend classes on Tuesdays, and the twelfth-grade girls are scheduled on Fridays. Although relatively few requests for excuses from swimming class have been received by Mr. Muller, the boys' physical education teacher, Miss Skolnik has received numerous requests. Miss Skolnik has requested a conference with Mr. Rothenberg, the director of physical education, to discuss the problem.

QUESTIONS

Should pupils be excused from swimming? Why are there more swimming excuses for girls than boys? What action should Miss Skolnik take to alleviate the situation?

ANALYSIS

There should be written policies and procedures for all excuses from any part of the physical education program. When pupils have permanent or prolonged excuses, it is desirable that a physician recommend to the chief school administrator the action he thinks is desirable. When pupils are permanently excused from swimming, they should still participate in other activities that have been adapted to meet their needs.

There are usually a greater number of requests for excuse from girls due to their menstrual period or because they are more concerned with personal grooming, particularly the appearance of their hair.

Miss Skolnik should ascertain from her girls why they want to be excused from swimming. In analyzing the situation, she may find that Friday is a poor day for the girls because it creates a grooming problem just before the weekend's social activities. Miss Skolnik should check with Mr. Rothenberg to see if she can schedule her twelfth-grade girls in the early part of the week.

DISCUSSION NOTES

**PERSONAL PRACTICE-TEACHING EXPERIENCE
RELATED TO TOPIC**

SELECTED REFERENCES

American Red Cross, *Instructors Manual: Lifesaving and Water Safety Courses*. Washington, D.C.: American National Red Cross, 1961.

──────, *Instructors Manual: Survival Swimming*, Washington, D.C.: American National Red Cross, 1961.

──────, *Lifesaving and Water Safety*. Garden City, N.Y.: Doubleday & Company, Inc., 1956.

──────, *Teaching Johnny to Swim*. Washington, D.C.: American National Red Cross, 1963.

ARMBRUSTER, DAVID, *Swimming and Diving*. St. Louis: C. V. Mosby Company, 1963.

GABRIELSON, M. A., *Aquatics Handbook*. Englewood Cliffs, N.J.: Prentice-Hall, Inc., 1960.

HARRIS, MARJORIE M., *Basic Swimming Analyzed*. Boston: Allyn and Bacon, Inc., 1970.

National Facilities Conference, *Planning Areas and Facilities for Health, Physical Education and Recreation*. Chicago, Ill.: Athletic Institute, 1965.

SPEARS, BETTY, *Fundamentals of Synchronized Swimming*. Minneapolis: Burgess Publishing Company, 1965.

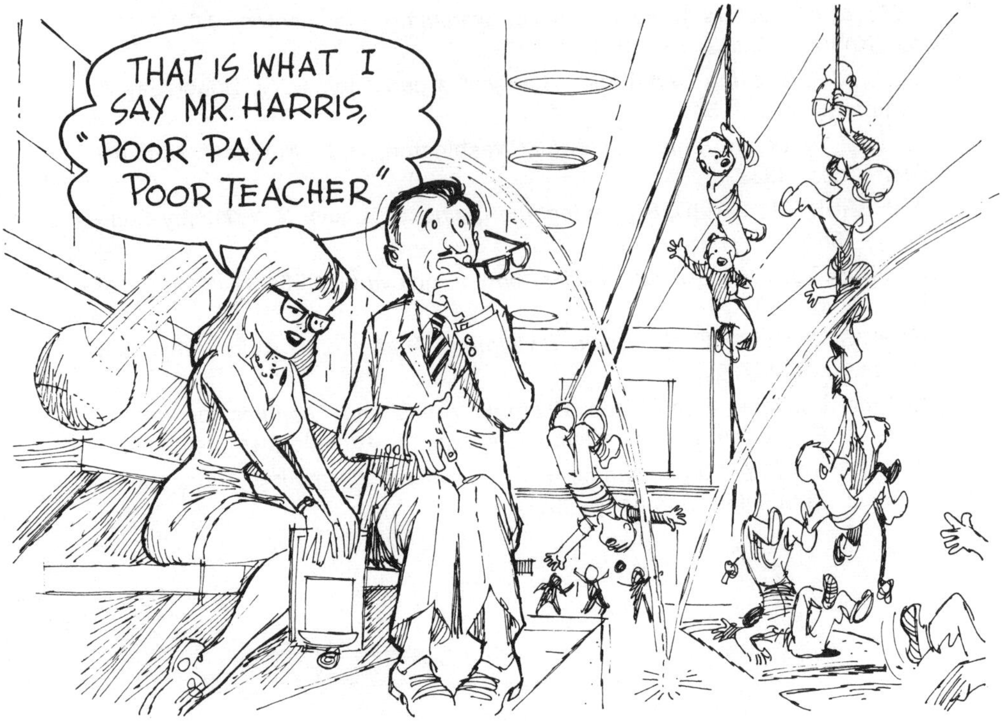
THAT IS WHAT I SAY MR. HARRIS, "POOR PAY, POOR TEACHER"

Personnel   CHAPTER 5

and

Scheduling

PERSONNEL

Although facilities, instructional supplies, and equipment are essential to an excellent program of physical education, it is the quality of personnel that determines the effectiveness of the program. The enthusiastic leadership of qualified personnel results in outstanding programs. Leadership, in physical education, means administration, supervision, and instruction.

ADMINISTRATIVE LEADERSHIP

The individual who is assigned administrative responsibilities in physical education must organize and implement the program on the basis of sound educational principles. He should possess human skills which permit him to communicate successfully and work cooperatively with others. His technical and conceptual skills should contribute to the achievement of both the general and specific objectives of the physical education curriculum.

In working with other staff members, the administrator must utilize his leadership ability in such a way that decisions are arrived at by the group through democratic procedures. Authority and responsibility should be delegated to staff members on the basis of their ability and experience, and they should be directly involved in determining departmental policies and procedures. Through democratic procedures the administrator develops the competencies of individual staff members and assists them in realizing the goals of the program. Occasionally, however, it will be necessary for the administrator to arrive at a final decision, particularly when the staff is unable to do so.

SUPERVISORY LEADERSHIP

One of the responsibilities of the administrator is supervision. In some school districts, the director of physical education assumes responsibility for the supervision of the program, while in other school systems there are separate supervisors who work with the director. The responsibilities of the director are more comprehensive, involving planning and directing the program. The supervisor is more closely concerned with the operation of the program and the teacher-pupil learning situation.

The supervisor should possess the same personal qualifications as other members of the staff. He should also have adequate successful teaching experience in schools, and one or more years of graduate study. Among other competencies he should be able to observe teachers, analyze their techniques, and evaluate their results. He should possess the ability to improve the teacher-pupil learning situation by constructive criticism.

PHYSICAL EDUCATION TEACHERS

The selection of physical education teachers should be based upon their personal and professional qualifications. They should have the same competence as other members of the faculty and be able to plan a comprehensive curriculum based upon the needs and interests of children.

Physical education teachers should possess the following personal qualifications:

- ☐ Faith in the worth of teaching and leadership
- ☐ Personal concern for the welfare of all people
- ☐ Respect for personality
- ☐ Understanding children, youth, and adults and appreciating their worth as citizens
- ☐ Social understanding and behavior
- ☐ Community-mindedness
- ☐ Interest in and aptitude for teaching and leading
- ☐ Above-average mental ability and common sense

PERSONNEL AND SCHEDULING

- ☐ Above-average health
- ☐ Voice of good quality and power, intelligently used
- ☐ Effective use of language
- ☐ A sense of humor
- ☐ Energy and enthusiasm sufficient to the requirements of effective leadership[1]

In addition to these personal qualifications, physical educators should have sufficient professional preparation to insure competency in technical skills and knowledge. Their competencies should include:

- ☐ Appreciation of the place and contribution of our schools in society, including the school in relation to the community
- ☐ Knowledge of the development and organization of our communities and our schools
- ☐ An understanding of child nature and development
- ☐ An understanding of the learning process and how to expedite it
- ☐ Skill in the adjustment of learning experiences to the nature and needs of people
- ☐ Knowledge and skill in the use of resource materials and of teaching and leadership aids
- ☐ Skill in the use of appropriate teaching and leadership techniques
- ☐ Proficiency in evaluating the outcomes of learning experiences
- ☐ Skill in making school and community life an experience in democratic living
- ☐ Mastery of basic and related materials involved in the area of leadership responsibility
- ☐ Knowledge and skill necessary to share in meeting common needs of people, without reference to the nature of the teaching or leadership assignment; for example, health education, physical education, and recreation needs, and guidance and counseling needs
- ☐ Skill in relating learning materials to the total learning experience of the individual
- ☐ Effectiveness in working with others, including pupils, colleagues, parents, and community
- ☐ A point of view in education and recreation that requires that practices be adjusted to all people and their welfare[2]

[1]*National Conference on Undergraduate Professional Preparation in Health Education, Physical Education and Recreation* (Chicago: The Athletic Institute, 1948), p. 7.
[2]*Ibid.*

CLASSROOM TEACHERS IN THE ELEMENTARY PHYSICAL EDUCATION PROGRAM

Although more and more physical education teachers are being employed by school systems to teach elementary school physical education, there are still many classroom teachers who assume responsibility for this area of the curriculum.

The elementary-classroom teacher in the primary grades of many schools is responsible for conducting the physical education program. In the intermediate grades there is a more highly specialized program of physical education activities, best taught by a physical education teacher who is more highly trained and skilled in physical education. Even in these grades the classroom teachers play a valuable role by assisting the physical education teacher and by teaching physical education to their classes on the days when the physical education teacher is not present.

CERTIFICATION OF TEACHERS

Most state education departments have specific regulations concerning the certification of physical education teachers. Professional preparation, in an accredited institution of higher learning having a teacher-education program in physical education, is usually required. The purpose of certification for teaching is to assure a school district that the individual is qualified and competent to teach physical education activities. In lawsuits involving negligence, the first question which must be answered is the competence of the person supervising at the time the accident occurred. If the person holds a teaching certificate, such license is prima facie evidence of competence.

IN-SERVICE EDUCATION

In order to produce more effective physical education teachers, develop their leadership ability, create *esprit de corps*, and guide their efforts toward the achievement of common goals, a continual program of in-service education is of the utmost importance. A variety of techniques may be employed in the conduct of in-service education. Some of these include graduate study, professional conferences and meetings, workshops, clinics, school visitations, staff meetings, and the reading of new books, professional journals and research reports.

RESPONSIBILITIES OF THE PHYSICAL EDUCATION TEACHER

The responsibilities of physical education teachers are numerous, and broad in scope. Depending upon the school system, physical educators may serve in either an administrative or teaching capacity. The larger the physical education program, the greater the need for personnel whose responsibility is solely administrative rather than instructional. Where the school system is small, the physical education teacher will usually assume responsibility for both administrative and teaching duties.

Besides teaching physical education classes, both men and women teachers may be required to conduct intramural and interscholastic athletic activities. Since intramurals should serve as the laboratory aspect of physical education class instruction and be available to all pupils regardless of their skill, this phase of the curriculum should not be adversely affected by the assignment of physical education personnel to the coaching of interscholastic athletic teams.

SCHEDULING

The utilization of teaching personnel and the scheduling of physical education classes are important administrative responsibilities that involve the total school program. The procedure by which physical education staff and classes are scheduled is indicative of the administrative philosophy of the school and will affect the quality of the program.

Scheduling is directly related to the total curriculum and must take into consideration such factors as: (1) the number of teaching stations available; (2) the size of the instructional staff available; and (3) the number of pupils to be scheduled.

Teaching stations. Adequate facilities should be provided in order to implement the curriculum. However, teaching stations, particularly indoors, are usually limited, and this necessitates an adjustment of activities to fit the space available. In making such adjustments, educational values must be weighed with respect to the objectives of the entire program.

A comprehensive survey should be made of all available facilities before developing a schedule. Sometimes a classroom may be used, particularly during inclement weather, to teach the knowledge-and-appreciation aspect of physical education. Sometimes facilities in the community, such as a bowling alley or skating rink, may be available for use.

Teaching staff. The utilization of the teaching staff should take into consideration such things as their own preferences, their ability to work with specific age groups, and their competencies in teaching various areas of the curriculum. Teachers who possess special skills—teaching body dynamics, games, self-testing activities, rhythms and dance, or aquatics—should be assigned accordingly. This opportunity will usually occur in larger schools, where there are more physical education teachers and a sufficient number and variety of teaching stations. Teachers who have an interest in younger boys and girls and relate positively with them should be assigned to teach physical education at the elementary level. Teachers who understand and communicate well with older students should teach in the secondary school. Every attempt should be made to schedule teachers in a manner which makes the best use of their abilities and results in a comprehensive curriculum which best meets the objectives of physical education.

Student body. In scheduling students, it is essential to see to it that everyone takes physical education. Students who are well enough to attend school should be assigned to physical education classes. These assignments, based upon the individual needs of students, will range from total participation to supervised rest. Consideration must be given to the assigning of outstanding students, in order to fulfill their needs, as well as to those boys and girls who have limited ability. Assignment of the latter group to study hall should not be considered a substitute for physical education.

The program should be organized with regard for the student's physical condition and therefore every pupil should have a medical examination. This should be done prior to his being scheduled for other subjects. In smaller schools, a small number of pupils would be classified for restricted activity, and scheduling a separate class for them would be difficult; in larger school districts the number may be sufficient to justify a separate, adapted class.

TYPES OF SCHEDULING

Traditional scheduling. Traditional scheduling, involving the same number of periods in each school day, of approximately the same amount of instructional time, has been used by many school administrators to assign pupils to classes. Such a system has not always proved to be successful, however, particularly with respect to physical education.

Modular scheduling. An innovation which has contributed to scheduling procedures is flexible, or "modular," scheduling. This type of scheduling is based on the premise that different types of courses require different kinds of time and that students having different abilities should not be kept together in a pattern determined by the format of the school day. By use of flexible scheduling, the instructional day is divided into a number of time units called "modules," rather than "periods." By adding one module to another, teachers may assemble their courses according to the time that is required for the specific educational activity planned. Through the use of computers, flexible scheduling may be established on a semester or yearly basis and can contribute to physical education by promoting greater utilization of facilities, increased student motivation, more efficient staff utilization, and individualized instruction.

The physical education staff should make the school administration aware of their departmental goals and of the best type of scheduling to achieve these goals. The staff should emphasize the specific problems inherent in scheduling pupils for physical education classes and should stress the rationale of basing the scheduling of classes on the number of teachers available, the number of teaching stations that may be utilized, and the number of students who must be scheduled. In this manner a quality curriculum, including progression of instruction, can be provided for all students.

personnel situations and analysis

FIRST SITUATION: INSUFFICIENT STAFF

The new superintendent of schools in Mineville has informed Mr. Bleecker, the director of physical education, that he wants all pupils in each of the six elementary schools to have a daily period of physical education. Mr. Bleecker is concerned about this request because he has only six physical education teachers assigned to the elementary schools, one in each school.

QUESTIONS

What should be the pupil-teacher ratio in order to offer a daily period of physical education to each pupil? What should be the pupil-teaching station ratio in order to offer a daily period of physical education to each pupil? Can the elementary-classroom teacher teach physical education?

ANALYSIS

When the physical education teachers do all the teaching of physical education in the elementary grades, a pupil-teacher ratio of 250 or less pupils per physical education teacher would permit a school to schedule a daily period of physical education for each pupil.

In order to have a daily period of physical education in the indoors teaching station, it is necessary to have approximately one teaching station for each 250 pupils. Since each school in Mineville has approximately 500 pupils, each school would need two indoors teaching stations. A teaching station indoors may be such areas as the gymnasium, swimming pool, playroom, and classroom.

In most states the elementary-classroom teacher is certified to teach elementary physical education. Often, however, because of a lack of interest and background, the elementary-classroom teacher is not well qualified to teach elementary physical education. Mr. Bleecker should ask the superintendent of schools for six more physical education teachers. A total of twelve physical education teachers in the six schools would allow each child to have a daily period of physical education. If he is unsuccessful in obtaining these additional teachers, he should have the superintendent of schools ask the elementary-school principals to have their classroom teachers supplement the physical education teaching.

SECOND SITUATION:
SHORTAGE OF TEACHERS FOR GIRLS

There is a shortage of women physical education teachers, and it is impossible for Mr. Duncan, the principal at Ridgeway High School, to employ one for the high-school girls' classes. He has received applications from three men physical education teachers and two women teachers who are not certified in physical education.

QUESTIONS

Who should teach physical education to high-school girls? What are some of the difficulties when men teach physical education to high-school girls? What are some of the problems when an uncertified woman teacher teaches physical education to high-school girls?

ANALYSIS

The person best qualified to teach physical education to high-school girls is the woman physical education teacher. She has a background of education specifically for this job. She knows the girls' activities and also appreciates and recognizes the differences in their anatomical, physiological, and emotional characteristics. The female physical education teacher is able to supervise the girls' dressing room and showering room. A woman physical education teacher can discuss freely the health problems of high-school girls.

When men teach physical education to high-school girls, the program is often basically a boys' activities program with boys' rules. It is impossible for the man to supervise the girls in the dressing room and showers, and girls do not feel free to discuss their health problems freely with men.

An uncertified woman teacher may lack the background to teach an adequate program, however. If she does not use good methods, much valuable time may be lost from the program. If she does not know proper "spotting" techniques, some pupil may be injured. Many uncertified female teachers can teach skills in only a few activities, and consequently the program is quite limited.

There is no reason why a man must always teach boys. If a man can teach girls in a coeducational class, he should be able to teach girls in a girls' class. Since Mr. Duncan has applications from three certified male physical education teachers, he should hire the man he thinks is the best teacher, rather than an uncertified female teacher.

THIRD SITUATION: SHORTAGE OF COACHES

The superintendent of schools has asked Mr. Snider, the director of physical education, to expand the number of interscholastic activities for high-school boys. There are three high-school men physical education teachers, each one of whom is responsible for one sport and assists with another sport, so that each teacher has one free season. Mr. Snider agrees that there should be more interscholastic teams but he also feels that each coach needs a free season.

QUESTIONS

How many different teams should one teacher coach? Who should coach the boys' high-school interscholastic teams? Should teachers receive additional compensation for coaching?

ANALYSIS

Probably the best arrangement is for a teacher to coach just one sport during the school year. In many small schools, however, if there is going to be a variety of interscholastic teams, it will be necessary for a teacher to coach during more than one sport season. It is generally agreed that the maximum coaching assignment for any one teacher should be only two sports seasons.

Some educators believe that the only teachers who should coach are the physical education teachers; others believe that any teacher should be able to coach. In order for most schools to have a variety of interscholastic teams, it is necessary to use both physical educators and other faculty members.

Since coaching is teaching, the teachers who coach should either receive additional funds for their coaching or compensatory time off during the regular school day. When additional monies are given for coaching, however, the school should have a consistent policy of giving additional monies to teachers who handle the school dramatics, bands, student council, or any other student activity that requires time beyond the regular school day.

Since Mr. Snider believes that a coach needs one free sports season, he should ask the superintendent for more physical education teachers or for the assignment of other faculty members who can coach certain sports. To expand the interscholastic program, it would be necessary to get more teachers who can coach, regardless of whether they are physical educators. If the problem in the past has been to get other teachers to coach, then maybe Mr. Snider should check the school policy about additional compensation for coaching.

FOURTH SITUATION:
THE LAY COACH

The local pharmacist is a former collegiate wrestler who is interested in starting a high-school team in Sprindale. The high-school principal has indicated that the school has nobody on the teaching staff who could coach the sport. The principal has also indicated that the school's policy is to have only certified teachers coach.

QUESTIONS

Should anybody coach high-school interscholastic teams? Should teachers have special certification as coaches in order to coach?

ANALYSIS

Coaching is teaching. Therefore, any person who coaches should be a certified teacher. Some states now have a certification for coaches, and the trend seems to be in this direction. Special certification would insure that all coaches have the necessary background to handle groups of boys in various activities. In several states where there is no special certification at present, many boys are being coached in contact sports such as football and wrestling by coaches who have never had a course in first aid.

Since the pharmacist probably does not have a teaching license, it is impossible for him to coach the wrestling team. The pharmacist may know the activity, but he may not know the boys. In other words, in coaching wrestling he would also be coaching boys. The school's policy is sound because the welfare of the boys must be the primary consideration. In order to expand the interscholastic teams to include wrestling, the principal should consider hiring a teacher with a background in wrestling.

FIFTH SITUATION: SHORTAGE OF STAFF

Mr. Browning is a new principal in LeRoy Elementary School, which has 500 pupils. He would like all pupils in grades 1 to 6 have a daily period of physical education. The practice in the past was to let the classroom teachers have a free period while their pupils are in physical education. There is only one physical education teacher available for full-time assignment in this school. Mr. Browning realizes that the classroom teachers need one free period daily, but he also realizes the need for all pupils to have a daily period of physical education.

QUESTIONS

Should the elementary-classroom teacher have a free period when her class has physical education? Should the elementary-classroom teacher have a free period when her class goes to other special subjects, such as music and art? Is it possible to have a daily period of physical education for each pupil and still allow the classroom teacher a free period each day?

ANALYSIS

The elementary-classroom teacher is occupied with many additional duties, including lunch room, bus, and playground supervision. For her own good physical and mental health, it is necessary for her to have some free time for rest and relaxation during the school day.

Some schools give the elementary-classroom teacher a free period when her pupils are having physical education. This is unfortunate, because physical education activities offer a unique opportunity for teachers to see children as they really are. Moreover, most elementary-classroom teachers are responsible for teaching some physical education even in schools with physical education teachers. In order to integrate and supplement what the physical education teacher is teaching, the classroom teacher should attend some of the classes taught by the physical educator. This would also be true of such subjects as music and art.

Mr. Browning could make it possible for all of the pupils in his school to have a daily period of physical education by having both the classroom teachers and the physical education teacher responsible for the teaching of physical education. By using the same procedures with both music and art, it would be possible to still give each elementary-classroom teacher one free period each day. For example, if the physical educator comes to the school on Monday, Wednesday, and Friday, the classroom teachers could get a free period on Monday and Friday one week, but attend the physical education classes on Wednesday. The next week they could get a free period on Wednesday, but attend physical education classes on Monday and Friday. The classroom teachers would teach their own physical education on Tuesday and Thursday. Following the same pattern of scheduling for music, art, and any other special subject, would permit the classroom teacher to have at least one free period daily, and would also keep him in touch with what the so-called "special" teachers were doing. In this manner the whole educational program for pupils can be better coordinated and integrated—and each pupil have a daily period of physical education.

SIXTH SITUATION:
SUPERVISION OF INTRAMURAL ACTIVITIES

The principals in the three elementary schools of Earlville are concerned because the three new physical education teachers go to Earlville High School after their last classes to assist in coaching varsity teams. Consequently, there are no intramural activities after school for the intermediate-grade boys and girls.

QUESTIONS

Should the elementary physical education teacher be responsible for the intramural activities for the elementary-grade pupils? Should the elementary physical education teacher be allowed to coach the interscholastic teams at the high school?

ANALYSIS

The elementary physical education teacher should be responsible for the intramural activities for the elementary-grade pupils, since this is an integral part of the physical education program. If these intramural activities are not offered to the intermediate-grade pupils, their physical education program is not a complete one.

In small school districts, where it is a problem to get sufficient staff to coach the boys' varsity high-school teams, the elementary physical education teacher is often asked to coach. If he is willing to coach and if it does not interfere with his prior responsibility to handle the elementary-grade intramural activities, this may be a satisfactory arrangement. This can be managed by having the elementary physical education teacher supervise the intramural activities directly after school. When he is through with this part of the program, he can go to the high school to coach. This arrangement works well in school districts where the elementary school day ends earlier than the secondary school, or in school districts where varsity teams practice at a later hour or after dinner. It must be kept in mind, however, that there is a limit to the physical stamina of a teacher.

DISCUSSION NOTES

**PERSONAL PRACTICE-TEACHING EXPERIENCE
RELATED TO TOPIC**

scheduling situations and analysis

**FIRST SITUATION:
INDOOR FACILITIES**

Mr. Jones, the physical education teacher, has been informed by his high-school principal that during the fall and spring he can have the pupils for a daily period of physical education. The principal said that this was possible because of the many outdoor physical education facilities that could be used, but added that it would be impossible during the winter months because of the lack of gymnasium space. He indicated to Mr. Jones that he would be willing to schedule physical education on a daily basis during the entire school year if somebody would show him how it could be done.

QUESTIONS

What adjustments can be made in the physical education program scheduling when there is inadequate gymnasium space? Are classrooms adequate for certain phases of physical education? Are there other resources within the community which may be used for teaching physical education indoors?

ANALYSIS

Mr. Jones should make a thorough search of available space in the school building that may be used for certain activities in physical education, such as large storerooms, wide corridors, and unused basement areas that can be ventilated properly. In these areas activities such as gymnastics, wrestling, dancing, archery, and riflery may be taught.

The knowledge-and-appreciation objective of the physical education program can best be taught in the classroom. Here such teaching aids as textbooks, films, and filmstrips may be used. The use of a classroom makes it possible for every pupil to have classes in physical education —even the medically excused youngsters will be able to take part. This also gives the physical education teacher a sound basis for marking pupils, and is more likely to result in the administrative granting of credit for physical education. Mr. Jones should check to see if classrooms can be made available for teaching physical education.

Mr. Jones should also check to see what community resources may be available for teaching physical education indoors, such as bowling, swimming, and skating facilities. These should be close to the school or valuable instructional time may be lost.

**SECOND SITUATION:
LARGE CLASSES**

Mr. Franklin, the principal of Greenleaf Elementary School, has scheduled a daily period of instruction in physical education for all pupils in grades 4, 5, and 6. In order to accomplish this, however, it was necessary to place 60 pupils in each class. Classes of this size adversely affect program and instruction. What should Mr. Jamison and Miss Richardson, the physical education teachers at Greenleaf Elementary School, do to improve the situation?

QUESTIONS

What is desirable class size in elementary physical education? Is it better to schedule pupils for fewer periods of instruction in physical education, thereby reducing class size, or to provide daily instruction to large classes? What are the legal implications when accidents occur in large physical education classes?

ANALYSIS

The size in an elementary physical education class should be the same as in any other class. When class size goes beyond 30 pupils it is extremely difficult for the classroom teacher or the physical education teacher to provide individual instruction.

Although it is desirable for all pupils to have a daily period of physical education, the class should be small enough so that adequate instruction in physical education may take place. It would be better for Mr. Jamison and Miss Richardson to request that pupils be scheduled for fewer classes per week, but of a size which permitted a program of physical education activities which would meet the pupils' individual needs and interests.

Negligence involves doing something which a reasonably prudent person should know or would know might lead to injury. In case of injury, the school may be proven negligent because a reasonably prudent person should know that scheduling an excessive number of elementary-grade pupils in a physical education class would be dangerous. For this reason alone, it is good policy to have the elementary physical education class size the same as other classes. It would be logical to assume that if the classroom teacher can adequately supervise the pupils in her classroom, the physical education teacher can adequately supervise the same number in most physical education activities. In certain situations, the number of pupils in a physical education class will of necessity be smaller, for reasons of safety. For example, a physical education teacher teaching swimming to nonswimmers should not be expected to teach the number of pupils generally found in a regular classroom.

THIRD SITUATION: SCHEDULING GIRLS' EXTRACURRICULAR ACTIVITIES

The women physical education teachers at Hackettstown High School have met with Mr. Grayson, the high-school principal, regarding equitable use of physical education facilities for boys and girls. The boys use the facilities for interscholastic athletics Monday through Thursday afternoon, while the girls are scheduled for extraclass activities on Friday afternoons.

QUESTIONS

Should the physical education facilities be scheduled equitably for both boys and girls? What adjustments should Mr. Grayson make in scheduling the high-school facilities so that the girls have a more adequate program of physical education?

ANALYSIS

The physical education facilities should be scheduled equitably for both boys and girls in order to meet the needs and interests of all pupils. It is just as important for the girls to have the opportunity to participate in a broad program of extraclass activities as it is for the boys.

In order to offer a more adequate program of extraclass activities for girls, Mr. Grayson should reschedule the use of the high-school facilities. He should consider scheduling girls' extraclass activities every day immediately after school for a specific period of time, and having the boys' extraclass activities follow. While the girls are using the facilities, the boys could do homework assignments, have conferences with teachers, or engage in other student activities.

**FOURTH SITUATION:
AGE GROUPING**

High-school pupils in the Lockwood School District are assigned to physical education classes according to the free periods in their schedule. This results in pupils of different grade levels being in the same physical education class and participating in the same physical activities. The physical education staff believes that such scheduling could adversely affect the safety of pupils and limit progression of instruction. What factors should be discussed in improving or eliminating this situation?

QUESTIONS

What adverse effects may result from pupils being scheduled for physical education during their free periods? What other methods can be used to schedule pupils for physical education?

ANALYSIS

When secondary-grade pupils are scheduled for physical education by free periods, classes are made up of pupils from different grades. In such situations, a single physical education class might contain pupils in grades 9 to 12. The differences in the size and strength of pupils in different grades could create a safety hazard.

When pupils are scheduled for physical education during free periods the teacher cannot teach by progression. He also must teach the same skills each year, to make sure each pupil has received adequate instruction in all activtities.

Other ways of grouping pupils for physical education include using the results of physical-fitness tests, skills tests, and anthropometric measures.

**FIFTH SITUATION:
MODULAR SCHEDULING**

The new principal at Bethlehem High School has talked to Mr. Shay, the director of physical education, about changing to modular scheduling. The high-school pupils at present are scheduled for three periods a week of 50 minutes each. The principal is suggesting that the pupils be scheduled for three 15-minute modules four days per week, and two 15-minute modules one day per week. Mr. Shay is deeply concerned as to what could be done in a 30-minute period.

QUESTIONS

Is it better to have fewer instructional periods of greater length per week or a greater number of instructional periods of shorter duration every week? What physical education activities could be taught in a 30-minute period?

ANALYSIS

In certain situations it would be better to have fewer and longer periods each week than to have a greater number of shorter periods. In schools where a few periods are scheduled for at least 60 minutes, there is more time for concentrated instruction and for dressing and showering.

However, at Bethlehem High School the present period is 50 minutes. As compared with the suggested 45 minutes, it is not enough additional time for extra instruction in activities or for dressing and showering. Moreover, the total amount of time would be greater for each pupil each week when shorter periods are scheduled. In this specific case, the total amount of time for the shorter periods would be 210 minutes per week, while the total amount of time for the longer periods is only 150 minutes per week.

There are certain parts of the class-instruction program for which it is not necessary to dress and shower. The classroom aspects of the physical education program, where the knowledge-and-appreciation aspects are taught, would not necessitate the pupils' dressing and showering and could well consume the 30-minute period which worries Mr. Shay. During this time, use could be made of audiovisual materials such as films, film strips, and textbooks.

Excellent use could be made of the shorter periods for orientation to physical fitness and for skills tests. This is also an excellent opportunity to administer tests of knowledge in physical education.

DISCUSSION NOTES

**PERSONAL PRACTICE-TEACHING EXPERIENCE
RELATED TO TOPIC**

SELECTED REFERENCES

ALLEN, DWIGHT W., "Elements of Scheduling a Flexible Curriculum," *Journal of Secondary Education,* XXXVIII (November, 1963), p. 84.

American Association for Health, Physical Education and Recreation, *Professional Preparation in Health Education, Physical Education and Recreation Education.* Washington, D.C.: National Education Association, 1962.

BUCHER, CHARLES A., *Administration of School and College Health and Physical Education Programs* (4th ed.). St. Louis: The C. V. Mosby Company, 1967.

BUSH, ROBERT N., "New Design for High School Education: Assuming a Flexible Schedule," *Bulletin of the National Association of Secondary School Principals,* May, 1962, p. 30.

CLEIN, MARVIN I., "A New Approach to the Physical Education Schedule," *Journal of Health, Physical Education and Recreation,* XXXIII (November, 1962), p. 34.

HAVEL, RICHARD C., and EMERY W. SEYMOUR, *Administration of Health, Physical Education and Recreation for Schools.* New York: The Ronald Press Company, 1961.

HUGHES, WILLIAM L., ESTHER FRENCH, and NELSON C. LEHSTEN, *Administration of Physical Education for Schools and Colleges.* New York: The Ronald Press Company, 1962.

IRWIN, L. W., and J. H. HUMPHREY, *Principles and Techniques of Supervision in Physical Education.* Dubuque: Wm. C. Brown Co., 1960.

NIXON, EUGENE W., and F. W. COZENS, *Introduction to Physical Education.* Philadelphia: W. B. Saunders Company, 1959.

NIXON, JOHN E., and ANN E. JEWITT, *Physical Education Curriculum.* New York: The Ronald Press Company, 1964.

VON BERGEN, ENID, and HARRY E. PIE, "Flexible Scheduling for Physical Education," *Journal of Health, Physical Education and Recreation,* XXXVIII (March, 1967), p. 29.

THIS **AUSTERITY BUDGET** IS REALLY KILLING US
OH, WOW!! ONLY **ONE** BOW AND **ONE** ARROW

Budget CHAPTER 6

In order for a program of education to be adequate, it is essential that a community have sufficient financial resources and be willing to spend them. Where such conditions exist a comprehensive instructional program and related services are usually provided. However, in school systems where funds are inadequate, instruction and services may be extremely limited or even nonexistent. Physical education, including athletics, are adversely affected or may not be provided at all. Physical education and intramural activities usually suffer as a result of insufficient staff, supplies, and equipment, and interschool athletics become dependent upon gate receipts.

SOURCES OF INCOME FOR PUBLIC EDUCATION

Funds for public education come primarily from a variety of governmental sources, including local, state, and federal allocations. Local taxes and state aid usually make up the greater amount of the support.

The financial responsibility for most public-school systems is undertaken by the local community, and the most common procedure for obtaining funds is through taxation. The procedures by which local taxes are levied and bond issues circulated is specifically determined by law. In recent years, the states have assumed a larger share of the financial responsibility for supporting their educational programs. State aid is determined by the ability of the municipality to pay its educational expenses, according to a formula established by the state. State school funds are secured through tax procedures similar to those used in local communities. Many states provide additional aid for improving such special school programs as vocational education, education for the physically, mentally, and emotionally handicapped pupils, and transportation of schoolchildren.

Federal aid to education has also increased considerably, and communities with programs that adhere to specific requirements receive federal funds for education. Besides special types of educational programs, federal aid is given for school lunches, vocational education, and the education of children of federal employees.

Other sources of income for financing local school programs of education are quite limited. Some private foundations interested in supporting worthwhile educational activities have given grants to school systems for implementing educational programs. Gifts and donations from private organizations and individuals may also be sources of income.

FINANCIAL MANAGEMENT IN PHYSICAL EDUCATION

An effective program of physical education requires one of the largest outlays in the educational budget. Such factors as facilities, personnel, supplies, and equipment contribute to the total cost. Because of the great expense involved, it is essential that there be appropriate financial management to insure that funds are used in the most advantageous manner.

There are a number of reasons why financial management is essential in the conduct of physical education programs, including: (1) to utilize funds in such a way as to provide for the best possible physical education program; (2) to make maximum use of factors such as facilities, personnel, supplies and equipment in achieving program objectives; (3) to avoid improper use and waste of funds; and (4) to involve all of the physical education staff in developing financial policies and procedures designed to give proper direction to the program.

BUDGETING FOR PHYSICAL EDUCATION AND ATHLETICS

The administration of a physical education program, including athletics, is an education enterprise. By necessity, however, it is also a business and must be conducted in a businesslike manner. This requires the determination of annual needs, income, and expenditures through the process of budgeting.

Budgeting is the development of a financial plan based upon work to be done and services to be carried out. To be educationally sound, all expenditures listed in the budget should be specifically related to the achievement of program objectives.

A budget is an organized statement of estimated receipts and expenditures. It is an estimate of income and revenues for a one-year period, referred to as the "fiscal year," which is not always the same as the school year. Although budgets are primarily concerned with a one-year period, they should also show long-term planning, indicating specific needs and costs, and provide for a well-planned program within the estimated income.

PURPOSES OF A BUDGET

A sound budget will:

- ☐ Indicate to the people of a school district what it costs in dollars and cents to provide a physical education program, including interschool athletics.
- ☐ Protect the continuation of this program for a specified period of time.
- ☐ Provide detailed information on physical education and athletic activities for which public funds are being used.
- ☐ Indicate where and when specific changes must be made to achieve certain objectives.
- ☐ Serve as a means of financial control.
- ☐ Serve as a basis for determining the amount of money that must be obtained from local taxation.
- ☐ Permit, with the approval of appropriate officials, the expenditure of funds for physical education.

PREPARING THE BUDGET

There are several plans for preparing budgets in public schools. Often the budget is prepared by the school principal and eventually submitted to the chief school officer for approval by the board of education. Or it may be developed by the chief school officer, who presents it to the principal for his comment and reaction. Sometimes the director of a specific school programs will develop a system-wide departmental budget and present it to the board of education through the chief school officer.

The physical education budget should be prepared cooperatively by the department administrator and his staff. When the budget has been approved, it should provide guidance and direction for the financial operation and administration of the department. The budget should then be continually evaluated to ascertain its effectiveness in achieving educational objectives.

BUDGET FORMAT

The format of the budget may vary. One budget might include a clear and concise introduction, designed to inform the school administration of the funds necessary to achieve the educational goals of the program. This could be followed by a comprehensive overview of the budget, including general expenditures and proposed revenues. The next section might include a detailed presentation of estimated expenditures and receipts, organized so as to permit others to understand the budget and analyze its cost factors. The final part of the budget could contain additional material intended to substantiate specific requests included in the budget.

In most budgets, the items are classified into three general categories: (1) instruction; (2) capital outlay; and (3) maintenance and operation. An item such as coaches' salaries would be included under instruction, a new swimming pool under capital outlay, and care of fields and grounds under maintenance and operation.

INCOME AND EXPENDITURES

Most school physical education programs receive finances from the general school fund, gate receipts, and activity fees. The general school fund is the major source of financial support, but in some schools gate receipts are a significant factor in financing the program of physical education. Schools also obtain funds from activity fees, the cost of admission to extra-class activities such as athletic events, plays, and concerts.

Expenditures for physical education usually involve capital outlays, such as for field renovations or a swimming pool; maintenance and operation outlays, such as for reconditioning uniforms and equipment, or for laundry service; and outlays for expendable equipment and supplies, such as for gymnastic apparatus or balls and bats.

ADOPTING THE BUDGET

The school budget for physical education is usually approved initially by the principal; then, if the school system has such a person, by the chief school officer; and finally, by the board of education.

A considerable amount of preparation should go into the final draft of the budget so that only minor changes are required for its adoption by the board of education. All financial requests should be educationally sound, and appropriate individuals and groups should be informed of the content of the budget before it is submitted. Such procedures tend to reduce difficulties when the budget is presented for adoption.

THE ADMINISTRATION OF THE BUDGET

When the budget has been approved, it is usually the responsibility of the director of the department to see that it is implemented. Before expending funds, he should be informed of the amount of money remaining in each category. The budget should serve as a guide for efficient operation and be closely followed, in order to serve its purpose.

FINANCIAL RECORDS

A detailed account of all monies expended for physical education is essential. The accounting system should include a record of all receipts and expenditures of funds. A periodic evaluation of the financial records should be conducted, to insure the proper management of funds. Some specific principles and policies concerning financial accounting include:

1. The administrative head has the final responsibility for accountability for all equipment and supplies in his or her organization.
2. Departments should establish and enforce policies covering loss, damage, theft, misappropriation, or destruction of equipment and supplies or other materials.
3. A system of accurate record keeping should be established and be uniform throughout the department.
4. Accountability should demonstrate the close relationship that exists between equipment and supplies and the program objectives.
5. A system of policies should be developed that will guarantee the proper use and protection of all equipment and supplies within the department.
6. The person to whom equipment and supplies are issued should be held accountable for these materials.
7. Accurate inventories are an essential to proper financial accounting.
8. A system of marking equipment and supplies as proof of ownership should be instituted.
9. A meaningful procedure should be established for the proper distribution of all equipment and supplies.
10. The discarding of equipment and supplies should take place only

in accordance with established procedures and by authorized persons.[1]

**THE BUDGET
FOR INTERSCHOLASTIC ATHLETICS**

The cost of conducting interschool athletic activities should be supported by the board of education in the same way as other areas of the curriculum. Such a policy would reduce many of the problems currently associated with interschool athletics and incorporate it as an educational activity within the total program of physical education.

The law permitting boards of education to expend funds for the support of interschool athletics varies in different states. Some states have ruled that boards of education have no legal power to expend money for interschool athletics since such activities are not a proper public-school activity within the scope of physical education as the term is stated in the law. Other states have interpreted interschool athletics as an integral part of the physical education program, and their boards of education do have legal power to provide financial support for these activities.

In situations where gate receipts, student athletic-association funds, and donations provide the major source of revenue for the conduct of interschool athletic activities, it is advisable to place such money under the supervision of the school district's business manager and make it part of the general school fund.

General school funds may be allocated to such activities as band, glee club, dramatics, and intramural and interschool athletics. Each activity develops its budget and receives appropriate financial support through the general fund. Among the advantages of such a system are:

1. Responsibility for disbursement of all school funds may be delegated to one individual.
2. It is in harmony with the plan of having all school activities under the general supervision of an all-school committee.
3. It enables the school administrator to have a composite picture of the general condition, financial and otherwise, of all the school activities.
4. It provides the possibility for a much more accurate audit of school activities funds than otherwise might be the case.

[1] *Equipment and Supplies for Athletics, Physical Education and Recreation* (Chicago: The Athletic Institute, 1960), p. 65.

5. The purposes for which expenditures are to be made may be more easily checked to ascertain if they are in accordance with authorization.
6. Local banking institutions usually will prefer a single school deposit account rather than separate ones for each school activity fund.
7. By its nature, the plan appeals to students and school patrons as being more business-like.[2]

In some school districts it is the policy that each high school in the district have its own athletic budget, based upon the estimated receipts and expenditures for each activity. In other school districts, particularly larger ones, it is often advantageous to allocate funds to each school on an equitable basis. Such a procedure is beneficial when the athletic funds of some schools are considerably greater than those of others. Other school districts have established policies whereby gate receipts become part of the general physical education budget and may be used to support all aspects of the physical education program.

SUPPLIES AND EQUIPMENT

Supplies are expendable materials that must be replaced quite often. Equipment is used over a period of years. Adequate supplies and equipment are essential in order to achieve program objectives, and they should be properly provided for in the budget.

The selection of supplies and equipment should be based upon the needs of the local school. The director, in cooperation with his physical education teachers and coaches, should select those items to be purchased. In large schools, a purchasing agent especially trained for such a responsibility usually does the purchasing. In small schools the director, teacher, or coach may do the buying, either directly or through the principal or business manager.

The principles governing the policies and procedures used in the selection and care of physical education supplies and equipment should:

1. Enable individuals and groups to participate satisfactorily in activities that serve their basic needs and interests and that contribute to personal growth and development.
2. Help in the attainment of the goals and objectives of the program in which the equipment and supplies are used, such as physical development, recreation, or training in skills.

[2]Charles E. Forsythe, *Administration of High School Athletics*, 3rd ed. (Englewood Cliffs, N.J.: Prentice-Hall, Inc., 1954), p. 250.

3. Help assure each individual or group using the supplies the maximum benefit and enjoyment attainable from participation in the activities.
4. Encourage the development and use of new types of equipment that foster imaginative play and creative forms of activity.
5. Make possible during any given activity period optimum participation by all members of the group.
6. Assure a maximum contribution to the health and safety of all persons involved in the activity.
7. Conform to widely accepted standards for the administration of athletic, physical education, and recreation programs.
8. Enable the individual or agency purchasing materials to realize for every dollar expended the fullest possible return as measured by the number of units or periods of satisfactory use.
9. Be administered according to a plan which provides that all persons involved in the selection, use, or care of equipment and supplies have clearly defined responsibilities and authority with respect to these functions.[3]

budget situations and analysis

**FIRST SITUATION:
FALLING GATE RECEIPTS**

Malverne High School had championship athletic teams for a number of years. Part of the funds obtained from gate receipts have been used to purchase equipment and supplies for the physical education program. For the past three years their teams have won only a few games and sufficient funds are not available to purchase the equipment and supplies needed for physical education class instruction. What steps should be taken to improve this situation?

QUESTIONS

Should physical education class instruction be supported by funds from interscholastic contests? Should interscholastic athletics be sup-

[3]*Equipment and Supplies for Athletics, Physical Education, and Recreation* (Chicago: The Athletic Institute, 1960), p. 3.

ported by the gate receipts of games? Should the interscholastic team that has the greatest gate receipts receive most of the athletic budget?

ANALYSIS

Physical education classes should be supported by funds from the regular school budget just as other subjects are. One part of the curriculum should not have to depend upon the success of another for financial support. Since physical education classes contribute to the education of every pupil, they should be included in each school budget. How much and what types of equipment, supplies, and apparatus are purchased for the physical education class-instruction program should not depend upon the success of any athletic team.

When competitive athletics are conducted in a desirable way, they can make a significant contribution to the education curriculum. Since interscholastic athletics are generally recognized as an integral part of the physical education program, they should be financially supported by funds of the board of education in the same way as other areas of the education curriculum. Where it is necessary to depend upon paid admissions for interscholastic contests, there will be a reflection of the public rather than the educational point of view. If athletics are ever going to reflect the views of education and not of the public, they must be independently financed.

In situations where gate receipts support all or part of the interscholastic program, funds should nevertheless be allocated to each athletic team on an equitable basis. The sport that receives the most in gate receipts should not necessarily receive the most funds. Other factors should be considered, such as the number of pupils served, the cost of supplies and equipment, and the educational value of each activity.

SECOND SITUATION: A TRAMPOLINE

Each year Mr. Grover and Miss Stuart, the physical education teachers at Knox Elementary School, have included a trampoline as one of the items in their budget request. Mr. Green, the principal, has refused to approve this budget item because he believes that it is too expensive and dangerous, and that pupils would receive limited use from it. Miss Stuart and Mr. Grover have arranged to meet with the principal to discuss the situation.

QUESTIONS

Is a trampoline a desirable piece of apparatus for elementary-school physical education classes? Who should make the final decision for approving items in the physical education budget?

ANALYSIS

The trampoline is a desirable piece of apparatus for elementary-grade pupils because it develops timing, coordination, a sense of balance, and body control. Although there is limited evidence that certain elements of danger are involved in trampolining, there is no conclusive evidence to show that this piece of equipment is undesirable. Most of the research has been done with high-school and college students, and there is little evidence to show that it is not desirable for elementary-grade pupils. It is no more dangerous than other pieces of apparatus in the elementary-school gymnasium if proper instruction is provided and safety procedures are followed.

It is true that usually only one pupil can use the trampoline at a time. However, the benefits gained from this piece of apparatus many not be obtainable on any other. For example, on no other piece of equipment can a pupil learn to control his body in the air as well as he can on a trampoline.

The cost of the trampoline is greater than most other pieces of apparatus, but its unique value justifies its expense.

The final decision for approving items in the physical education budget should rest with Mr. Green, the principal. However, since Miss Stuart and Mr. Grover are the educational specialists in this area, they should be consulted. In their conference with Mr. Green, the physical education teachers should present justification for their request of the trampoline.

THIRD SITUATION:
SUPPLIES AND EQUIPMENT

The physical education staff at the new Glenville Elementary School has been allocated a specific amount of money for supplies and equipment. In order to provide the best program possible within the budget allocation, what type and amount of supplies should be purchased by the physical education staff?

QUESTIONS

Is it possible to conduct a satisfactory program of physical education with little or no supplies or equipment? What priorities should be considered when purchasing supplies and equipment? What effect does available storage space have on the purchase of supplies and equipment? What effect does the number of pupils have on the purchase of supplies and equipment?

ANALYSIS

Although a few physical education activities can be taught without some supplies and equipment, it is generally believed that in order to conduct a satisfactory program it is necessary to have a sufficient number and variety of supplies and equipment.

The physical education staff should determine whether the present supplies and equipment are adequate for the program. If there is a shortage of materials, priority should be given to purchasing necessary supplies and equipment for activities which presently are being taught.

There should be sufficient storage space for all indoor and outdoor supplies and equipment to insure its being kept in a good and safe condition. If there are insufficient areas for storage, it may be necessary to limit the type and amount of supplies and equipment until adequate space is obtained. When there is a limited area for storage, first consideration should be given to purchasing supplies and equipment that require little or no storage space. Such pieces of apparatus as ropes and rings require no special storage space, while a trampoline and parallel bars require considerable space.

The number of pupils who use the supplies and equipment will help determine the amount needed. This will also determine the types purchased in order to permit maximum participation. When all pupils participate, the individual pupil's needs and interests are met and a contribution is made to his personal growth and development.

FOURTH SITUATION: LAUNDRY EQUIPMENT

Mr. Johnson, the director of health, physical education and recreation at Park Ridge Central Schools, has requested that a laundry unit be included in the plans for the new high school. Dr. Benson, the superintendent of schools, believes it would be too expensive and is not necessary. What reasons should Mr. Johnson present in attempting to show the superintendent the benefits of a school laundry?

QUESTIONS

How much space is required to house a school laundry? Does a school laundry save money for a school district? What necessary services can a school laundry provide? In addition to saving money, what additional benefits does a school laundry provide?

ANALYSIS

In planning new facilities, there is always concern about the space needed for the various areas of an educational program. It is a misconception that school laundries require considerable space. It is possible for smaller schools to have adequate laundry facilities in a room 12 by 10 feet, and for larger schools to have their laundry facilities in a room 20 by 20 feet. In both of these rooms there will be adequate space for the laundry tray, washer-extractor, tumbler, and storage bins or shelves.

A considerable amount of money can be saved when a school district has its own laundry because: (1) launderable items are less costly than items that are dry cleaned; (2) laundry items are kept in the school, with less loss; (3) and laundry items last longer because the school can control the laundering procedures. It has been the experience of schools with their own laundries that they have saved enough money in one year to pay for the equipment.

In addition to the laundering of towels and uniforms in physical education and athletics, a school laundry can serve the homemaking program and cafeteria, for example. Often there are emergencies or exceptional demands that are more adequately met when a school has its own laundry.

One of the greatest benefits that a school laundry provides is insuring that all pupils will have a clean uniform and towel when they are participating in physical education and athletics. This will help all pupils maintain desirable health practices.

FIFTH SITUATION:
UNBUDGETED EQUIPMENT

The budgeted allocation for physical education supplies and equipment has been expended. Funds were not available to purchase a balance beam and vaulting box for use in gymnastics. The physical education staff at Howe Junior High School has obtained the cooperation of the industrial-arts department to construct these pieces of apparatus.

QUESTIONS

Are the balance beam and vaulting box necessary for teaching a broad program of gymnastics? Are there other means of getting funds for the apparatus? Should the industrial-arts department construct gymnasium apparatus?

ANALYSIS

It is necessary to have several different pieces of apparatus in order to teach a broad program of gymnastics. The balance beam and the vaulting box are recognized as essential pieces of equipment in this aspect of the physical education program. The value of the balance beam is that it provides opportunities for pupils to develop coordination, concentration, balance, and dexterity. The vaulting box is probably the most natural and appealing to most pupils because running and leaping are fundamental motor skills. It is probably the most versatile vaulting apparatus because it can be used lengthwise, sidewise, or diagonally, and its height can be easily adjusted to meet the needs of various pupils.

There are several ways of obtaining monies for the purchase of necessary gymnasium apparatus, depending upon the school and community. In some school districts where there are active Parent-Teachers Associations, funds are given to the schools for the purchase of such equipment. Individual citizens who are interested in the physical education program sometimes donate money specifically for it. Commercial and industrial businesses may sometimes make contributions to schools for the purchase of necessary teaching supplies and equipment. In communities where there are active service clubs, these often make contributions to school districts when there is a need. The physical education staff at Howe Junior High School should confer with their principal to see if any funds are available from such sources.

In school districts where there are adequate industrial-arts departments it may be possible to construct gymnasium apparatus that would meet manufacturers' specifications. When using such equipment, the staff should test it thoroughly before allowing pupils to use it. However, it is more desirable to purchase gymnasium apparatus from a recognized equipment company whose materials have been tested and whose products meet specific safety standards.

SIXTH SITUATION: BUDGET CUTS

Dr. Fleming, superintendent of schools in Sackett County, has informed each of the elementary-school principals that they must cut their total budget by $300. Mr. Bennett, principal of the Riverside Elementary School, has eliminated the entire $300 budget request which Mr. Cartwright, the director of health, physical education and recreation, included in his physical education budget.

QUESTIONS

When adjustments must be made in a budget, should monies allocated for one program be eliminated? Who should determine what changes should be made when adjusting budgets?

ANALYSIS

Every program in the curriculum makes a contribution to the total education of all pupils, and so should receive some money for necessary teaching supplies and equipment. Consequently, if a budget has to be trimmed, it would be more educationally sound to reduce monies for each program rather than eliminate the total funds allocated for one program. In physical education, if necessary teaching supplies and equipment are not available there is a loss of valuable instructional time, pupil participation is limited, there is a decrease in teaching efficiency, and a great loss of interest on the part of both pupils and teachers.

It is sound administrative practice to include the personnel directly responsible for the program of physical education in determining the supplies and equipment needed to carry on a program of activities which meets the needs and interests of pupils. Any changes that affect physical education items in the budget should involve appropriate physical education staff.

DISCUSSION NOTES

PERSONAL PRACTICE TEACHING EXPERIENCE RELATED TO TOPIC

SELECTED REFERENCES

BUCHER, CHARLES A., *Administration of School and College Health and Physical Education Programs.* St. Louis: The C. V. Mosby Company, 1967.

GEORGE, JACK F., and HARRY A. LEHMANN, *School Athletic Administration.* New York: Harper & Row, Publishers, Incorporated, 1966.

HAVEL, RICHARD C., and EMERY W. SEYMOUR, *Administration of Health, Physical Education and Recreation for Schools.* New York: The Ronald Press Company, 1961.

MORT, PAUL R., WALTER C. RENSSER, and JOHN W. POLLEY, *Public School Finance.* New York: McGraw-Hill Book Company, 1960.

The Athletic Institute, *Equipment and Supplies for Athletics, Physical Education and Recreation.* Chicago, 1970.

ACE
ACE CONSTRUCTI
HIGH
GYMNASIUM
OH NO!! THE BLUEPRINTS MUST HAVE BEEN FOLDED WRONG!

Facilities CHAPTER 7

The personnel responsible for the organization, administration and conduct of the physical education program has an important role in the development of functional facilities that are adequate for the program. These facilities should be based on: (1) the physical education activities, which are designed to meet the interests and needs of the pupils; (2) the amount of time that the pupils spend in class instruction, intramurals, extramurals, and interscholastics; (3) the ultimate enrollment of the school; and (4) the official size of playing areas.

The facilities should be planned so that they are functional and take into consideration the various needs for organized recreation. Such planning would provide facilities for both physical education and recreational programs and would spread the cost of this part of the modern school plant. The use of the elementary school as a neighborhood center and the secondary school as a community center has saved the cost of constructing separate recreation centers in many communities.

INDOOR FACILITIES

In planning the indoor facilities with which to administer and carry on the physical education program, basic consideration should be given to the following areas: gymnasium, swimming pool, apparatus storage room, boys' dressing room and showering rooms, girls' dressing room and showering rooms, adapted activities room, physical education office, team room, equipment-drying room, laundry room, supply-storage room, and classroom.

TEACHING STATIONS

A teaching station is defined as a room that can be regularly scheduled for a class under the direction of a teacher. Wise planning establishes some priority for the types of teaching stations. For the school which needs three stations, it would be wise to give first priority to a gymnasium with a folding partition and two stations, and second priority to a pool as the third station. The next priority, if a swimming pool is not possible, is a single teaching station.

The number of teaching stations needed for a school will depend upon:

- ☐ The ultimate enrollment of the school.
- ☐ The number of pupils in a physical education class.
- ☐ The number of periods a teaching station is scheduled for use per week.
- ☐ The number of periods each pupil is scheduled for physical education per week.
- ☐ The number of activities and pupils in the extra-class program.

GYMNASIUM

The gymnasium should be at or slightly above ground level. The auxiliary facilities, when possible, should be adjacent and at the same level. This unit should be readily accessible from the rest of the building and from the outdoor physical education facilities. The facilities should be near the auditorium and cafeteria in order that they may be used in conjunction with community recreational activities without opening the entire building.

Gymnasium Floor Space. It will be necessary to provide, within the floor space, as many separate class areas as are needed for the simultaneous activities of different physical education classes, and of a size which will accommodate a maximum-size class of 40 pupils. In addition to these areas there should be a reasonable amount of seating space for spectators when the physical education areas are used for interscholastic sports.

In *elementary schools* requiring a single teaching station, the minimum floor space should be 40 by 60 feet. Where two such areas are necessary, the space may be in the form of two areas each 40 by 60 feet, or one space 60 by 80 feet which is divisible by a folding partition. If it is anticipated that the school will serve as a neighborhood recreation center, a larger area should be provided to accommodate such activities as basketball, badminton and volleyball.

In *secondary schools* where the program and enrollment require only a single teaching station, a minimum floor space 52 by 84 feet should be planned. An area 84 by 104 feet of clear floor space, exclusive of folded-back bleachers, will give two teaching stations of sufficient size. It should be equipped with a motor-driven folding partition which is soundproof and extends from floor to ceiling. Curtains and nets in place of the partition are inadequate and not desirable. The folding bleachers will provide substantial seating capacity for spectator sports in a minimum of additional space, as compared with fixed seating.

When the program and enrollment of the school require more than two teaching areas, the additional facilities may be secured by extending the gymnasium area to provide another teaching station or by adding small group-activity rooms.

An additional teaching station may be gained by constructing a swimming pool. A reasonable pool size, and one which will accommodate interscholastic swimming competition, is 42 by 75 feet 1 inch in length.

GYMNASIUM TREATMENT

The finish of the gymnasium should be in keeping with the purpose of the room. There is no need for elaborate appointments. The room should be simple. It must lend itself to hard, vigorous usage. The walls should be light in color, and smooth and regular, with no projections or sharp corners that may be hazardous to pupils. Care should be taken to insure that doors and doorways are not so located as to be a safety hazard. For example, doors in the center of the end walls of the gymnasium are a hazard to those using the gymnasium for active games as well as to those passing in the corridor on the opposite side of the doors. Corner locations are preferable. Acoustical treatment is imperative.

The height of the gymnasium proper should never be less than 18 feet; and a maximum of 20 to 22 feet is preferable. If beams are left exposed, equipment can be suspended. If the ceiling is to be furred below the structural members, the attachment of suspended equipment should be planned and eyebolts provided during the construction of the room. Some schools have found that eyebolts provided in each corner of the gymnasium during its construction have proven useful when decorating the room for school social events. When equipment which will require fastening to the wall or floor, such as horizontal bars and volleyball standards, is to be used, a layout of its placement should be made so that wall boards and floor sockets can be provided at the time of construction.

When the design of the building will permit, high bilateral lighting (light coming from high windows on both sides of the gymnasium) is desirable. In order that the gymnasium wall may be used for rebounding in such activities as handball, fielding a softball, and handling a basketball, window sills should be placed 10 feet above the floor. If possible, they should be arranged so that pupils using the basketball backboards in the daytime are not looking up into the windows. If this arrangement is not possible, they should be provided with some type of shade or constructed of diffusing glass to eliminate glare. Windows divided into small panes of heavy plate or tempered plate glass are desirable, as window guards are not then needed. The elimination of guards makes it easier to open the windows.

The generally preferred flooring for the gymnasium is first-quality, northern, hard-strip maple, laid on sleepers. It makes a floor that is resilient, durable, smooth, and easily cleaned. The floor should always be designed so that it can be ventilated underneath to prevent dry rot. Experience has proved that the gymnasium floor should never be located below grade level.

A finish especially designed for gymnasiums should be used, rather than ordinary floor finishes or varnishes. Floor markings should be worked out according to the games and activities to be played. The lines should be painted on the gymnasium floor in differentiating colors and varying widths before the final finish is applied. A minimum of 3 feet should be allowed for a safety zone between the adjacent lines of the playing areas and between the lines of the playing areas and the walls of the gymnasium. A suggested scheme of colors and width of lines is:

Badminton	— Red	— 1½ inches wide
Basketball	— Black	— 2 inches wide
Shuffleboard	— Yellow	— 1½ inches wide
Volleyball	— Green	— 2 inches wide
Indoor Baseball	— Blue	— 2 inches wide
Circle Games	— Orange	— 2 inches wide

Drinking fountains should be located in the corridors, convenient to the doors leading from the gymnasium. A safety hazard is involved in placing fountains in the gymnasium because of the inevitable sloshing of water.

The number, size, and details of exit doors should meet the current Building Exit Code of the National Fire Protection Association.

THE SMALL GROUP-ACTIVITY ROOM AND AUXILIARY GYMNASIUM

These rooms will accommodate apparatus, stunts and tumbling, wrestling, adapted activities and rhythms and dance. The size of the groups, however, will be limited. In elementary schools these rooms should be at least 36 by 52 feet, with a minimum height of 12 feet. In secondary schools, they should be at least 40 by 60 feet, with a minimum height of 14 feet.

Bulletin Boards. Bulletin boards should be provided and placed in a well-lit area near the dressing rooms and showering rooms where they may readily be seen by all pupils. Glass-covered boards make for a neat appearance and protect the boards from being defaced.

Electrical Installation. Provision should be made for the installation of a separate public-address system, picture projectors, radio, television, record players, cleaning machines, and electric scoreboards. The controls for the gymnasium lighting should be conveniently located, recessed, and keyed.

SWIMMING POOL

The swimming pool should be planned and constructed in accordance with the desires and needs of the school and community it is to serve. Since swimming is an integral part of the physical education program, the pool site should be integrated with the other physical education facilities. Building costs can be saved by having such facilities as the lockers, showers, toilets, and drying rooms that service the regular physical education classes also be used by the swimming groups, although in large schools there may be merit in having swimming pools with their own dressing and showering facilities. In elementary schools, an instructional pool of 3 to 4 feet of constant depth, 30 feet in width, and 60 feet in length will save considerable cost.

The slope of the bottom of the pool should be governed by the purposes for which it will be used. The slope will determine how much of the pool can be used for instructional purposes and how much will be available for safe diving. For safety, the slope should be a maximum of 1 foot for every 15 feet.

Approximately 60 per cent of the pool area should be shallow water in order to provide enough area to teach beginning swimmers. When the program includes lifesaving, synchronized swimming, and other deep water skills, 40 per cent of the pool area should be deeper water.

There should be adequate floor space around the pool for a deck area. This serves as a place for rest periods and for the conduct of land drills and demonstrations. The surface in this area should be non-slip, and deck drains should be properly spaced throughout.

All pool markings should be imbedded in the building materials so that they are permanent. The lane markings on the bottom of the pool should be of a dark color and designed according to regulations governing swimming competition.

The number and height of the diving boards will be determined by the size of the pool, the depth of the water, and the height of the ceiling. Recessed ladders should be located at the corners of the pool, with handrails.

There should be an office with a vision panel or a small glass enclosed cubicle adjacent to the pool deck. It should have a clear, unobstructed view of the entire swimming area. Here such things as teaching materials, record player, and personal belongings may be housed. As an indispensable safety measure, this office or cubicle should have a telephone for direct outside calls.

DRESSING ROOMS AND SHOWERING ROOMS

Since dressing and showering are recognized as integral parts of the health and physical education programs, it is desirable that pupils in the elementary schools have an opportunity to dress and shower during the physical education class and extra-class program. There should be separate rooms for boys and girls so that they can be used simultaneously during coeducational activities.

Eight to twelve-year-old pupils are ready for showering and should not be denied the opportunity of establishing this desirable health practice. The health and safety of pupils should be a primary concern of the school, and provision should be made for third and fourth-grade pupils to dress and shower. When dressing and showering are introduced in these grades, there are usually fewer problems with this part of the program in junior and senior-high school.

Boys' Dressing Room and Showers. The location and size of the boys' dressing room and showers, and the arrangement of the facilities within the rooms, are of great importance in the administration of the physical education program of the school.

The preferred location is on the same floor as the gymnasium and adjacent to it, so that pupils can pass directly to and from the gymnasium without going into the corridors of the school. It is also desirable that pupils be able to pass directly between the dressing room and the outside playing fields without using the general school corridors. It should also be possible to enter the dressing room from the corridor without going into the gymnasium. If a team room is provided, it should be possible to enter it directly from the playing field.

Lockers should be of two types, the gymnasium suit or storage locker and the street clothes or dressing locker. For hygienic reasons a storage locker 9 by 12 by 24 inches, or 9 by 12 by 30 inches is preferred to the box-type locker. In a locker of this length it is possible to hang up the physical education uniform and thereby insure drying and ventilation. A dressing locker 12 by 12 by 60 inches, or 12 by 12 by 72 inches, is satisfactory.

One storage locker must be provided for each boy using the dressing room, and one dressing locker is required for each boy in the maximum-size physical education class. In addition, there should be a sufficient number of dressing lockers to hold the uniforms of the largest squad in the various interscholastic sports in which the school competes. These lockers may be housed in a space set aside for them in the dressing room or in a separate team room adjacent to the body-drying space. When a team room is provided, a small section of it may be partitioned off to serve as a drying room for the uniforms. This room should have positive ventilation and sufficient heat to insure drying.

The dressing lockers used by the physical education classes should be interspersed equally among the rows of storage lockers. The rows of lockers should not be closer than 5 feet face to face. All lockers should be mounted on a cove masonry base. The locker arrangement within the room should be such as to facilitate the supervision of all activity therein from the physical education office through a glass panel provided for that purpose.

Another type of storage is handled through a basket system. Several types have been used successfully, such as the post-office basket, basket storage on movable trucks, and attendant-operated.

Fixed benches should be provided. Mirrors should be conveniently located in several places around the dressing room. A drinking fountain should be installed.

If the dressing facilities are to be used by adults, the only additional requirement is that each adult be provided with a storage locker.

In order to determine the area needed for the dressing room, it is necessary to know the following facts: (1) the total number of different pupils who will be using the dressing room; (2) the number of storage lockers in each unit of the battery arrangement; (3) the peak-load of pupils using the dressing room at one time; and (4) the area required for each battery of lockers.

The showering room may have either the wall-type group shower arrangement or the walk-around arrangement. In either case there must be enough shower heads to accommodate the largest physical education class that will result from the school's enrollment. One vandal-proof shower head should be planned for each four boys in the class if the group-shower arrangement is used and one for each three boys if the walk-around arrangement is used. Shower heads should be at least 4 feet apart and not more than 5 feet above the floor in secondary schools. Elementary-school showers should be between 48 and 54 inches from the floor.

In large showering rooms having the group-shower arrangement, better use can be made of the center area by having a dwarf-type central wall, 5 to 6 feet high, with shower heads on both sides.

A control for the water supply should be placed outside of the shower room where it may be operated by the teacher. Where group showers are used, each shower head should be independently controlled. Where the walk-around shower is used, at least one shower head should be equipped for independent control. The remainder of the shower heads should be adjusted so that the temperature of the water will vary from warm to tepid to cool. The water temperature should never exceed 110° F.

A liquid-soap dispenser outlet may be located at each shower head in the group shower. About three soap outlets should be distributed along the "in" side of the walk-around shower and at least two at the turn before starting down the "out" side. These soap outlets should be supplied from a central reservoir of sufficient size to accommodate a day's supply of soap.

The floor and walls of the showering room should be constructed of an impervious material. The material used for the floor should be abrasive or nonskid as well. The ceiling and walls should be left unpainted. Sufficient drains should be provided, and so located that no pupil need stand in or walk through waste water.

The body-drying space is an essential adjunct to the showering space. It should be so located that the pupils must pass through it after showering, before they enter the dressing room proper. It should be large enough to accommodate as many pupils as will be in the shower at one time. Ordinarily, 150 to 200 square feet of floor space will be adequate. Towel service is desirable and is found in more and more schools. When towel service is to be offered, a towel-distribution cubicle with a window opening into the body-drying space should be provided. Sufficient hooks for hanging up towels should be provided around the wall of the body-drying space. A hamper or used-towel receptacle is needed at or near the opening between the body-drying space and the dressing room.

The wall between the drying room and the dressing room may be of the dwarf type, 4 to 6 feet high. The opening between the body-drying space and the dressing space should be at least 4 feet wide, to permit pupils to pass each other. The opening between the body-drying space and the shower space should be of like width and should contain a sill 6 inches high, to prevent water on the floor of the shower space from running into the body-drying space. Drains should be located in the body-drying space so that water dripping from the body will be carried away and not tracked into the dressing room.

Girls' Dressing Room and Showering Rooms. Everything that has been said concerning the dressing, showering, and drying space for boys may be repeated for the facilities for girls. In order to meet the concern of some parents about girls using group showers, there should also be one or two individual shower and dressing-booth cubicles, according to the size of the school. However, most of the showers should be of the group type because they are less expensive to install, easier to supervise, and easier to keep clean. Shower heads should be located not more than 4 feet, 6 inches from the floor. Several mirrors should be provided so the girls can complete their grooming.

Toilets. Toilets should always be located in the dressing room proper, not in the body-drying space. It should not be necessary for pupils to enter either the body-drying space or shower space except when undressed for the shower. There should be a minimum of two water closets and one lavatory in the girls' dressing room for a class of 40 pupils. In the boys' dressing room there should be a minimum of one water closet, one urinal, and one lavatory for a class of 40 pupils.

The lighting of the showers and the body-drying and dressing rooms should be a minimum of 5 foot-candles (maintained), and the switch for the lights of the showers and body-drying space should be located in the dressing room. The rooms should be positively ventilated, and heated to 78° F.

Team Dressing Room. In the senior-high school it is desirable to have a separate home-team dressing room for boys on the interscholastic squads. This room should be designed so that the regular showers are directly accessible, and it should contain full-length lockers. In order to ascertain the area needed for this room, it is necessary to know the following facts: (1) the total number of different pupils that will be using the team room; (2) the area required for each locker; and (3) the peak load of pupils using the team room at one time.

Equipment Drying Room. The drying room for equipment should be adjacent to the team room. It should be of sufficient size to take care of the peak load of equipment to be dried at one time. There should be sufficient circulation of air at a high temperature, in order to insure proper drying of the equipment.

LAUNDRY ROOM

The laundry room should be of sufficient size to accommodate the equipment. It is much better to have the commercial rather than the home type, including the washer and dryer. In addition to towels, physical education uniforms can be washed, including many items of clothing used in interscholastic activities that are frequently sent out to be dry cleaned. Laundry from other areas, such as the cafeteria, can also be washed in this room.

APPARATUS AND SUPPLY STORAGE

Good design of the apparatus and supply storage room will ensure that it has three essential characteristics: easy access from the gymnasium floor; door openings wide enough to permit the moving of equipment from the gymnasium floor into the storage space with ease; and enough space to accommodate all the movable equipment.

Preferably, the apparatus and supply storage room should be adjacent to the gymnasium. When it is necessary to locate the apparatus storage room across a corridor from the gymnasium, care should be taken that the doors of the two rooms are directly opposite. Six-foot doors with a flush threshold are needed to permit the movement of equipment from the gymnasium to the storage space. Consideration should be given to having an overhead door, so that when the room is being used the door is neither an obstacle nor a hazard.

The usual apparatus and supplies requiring storage space include parallel bars, horse, buck, springboard, beat board, volleyball standards and nets, horizontal bars, stall bar benches, mats, testing equipment, archery targets, out-of-season uniforms and equipment, and so on. A room with 300 to 400 square feet of floor space is adequate for secondary schools. A room with 200 to 225 square feet of floor space should provide sufficient storage space for elementary schools.

The apparatus and supply storage room should be well lighted and should have positive ventilation. It should be equipped with cabinets and bins in which those articles of supplies that are in daily use, such as volleyballs, basketballs, indoor baseballs, and bats, may be kept. These facilities should be provided with locks. Provision should also be made for storing equipment and supplies which have not been put into use. Built-in shelves are generally recommended for this type of storage.

CLASSROOM

It is desirable to have available at least one regular classroom equipped with the usual teaching aids as well as for the use of audio-visual materials. This room is a desirable area to teach the knowledge-and-appreciation aspects of physical education. The utilization of such a room saves valuable instructional time in the gymnasium and on the playing fields.

PHYSICAL EDUCATION OFFICES

There should be separate offices for men and women physical education teachers. If offices are provided for individual teachers, there should be 100 to 130 square feet of space; when group offices are needed, there should be 70 to 90 square feet of space for each teacher. In large schools, consideration should be given to having group offices for the several teachers and a separate office for the chairman or department head. There should be enough room for desks and files, and limited cabinet space for the storage of some instructional supplies, such as basketballs, footballs, baseballs, volleyballs, bats, and tennis rackets. There should be some dressing lockers for physical education teachers, other teachers who are coaching, and athletic officials.

Separate showers and toilet facilities for the teachers are desirable. These rooms should be adequately lighted, heated, and ventilated. The physical education offices should be proximate to the gymnasium and the dressing room, and should enter upon both of these rooms.

Vision panels between the offices and the dressing rooms and showering rooms, and also between the offices and the indoor teaching stations, are desirable because they provide additional safety and supervision of classes when the teacher is called to his office.

OUTDOOR FACILITIES

In planning the outdoor facilities to serve the pupils in a school, it should be kept in mind that the modern school has two major needs: (1) to provide the physical education facilities that will permit the program to meet the needs and interests of all pupils during the school day; and (2) to provide the physical education and recreation facilities that meet the needs and interests of all pupils participating in activities after school hours. Such planning is sound because it provides for maximum utilization of all facilities and allows for professional supervision and economical operation.

The outdoor physical education and recreation areas should be planned according to the program offered and the number of pupils to be served during the periods of peak or maximum load. The program, since it is based on the pupils' needs and interests, is of primary importance. Regardless of the number of pupils to be served, the program dictates the necessity of having certain areas of more or less definite size.

The National Facilities Conference on Planning Areas and Facilities for Health, Physical Education, and Recreation proposes standards which should be useful in getting functionally planned and more adequate facilities for neighborhoods and communities. The park-school is a school building on a park site which is designed to function as a center for programs of education and recreation throughout the year. The standards recommended for park-schools are as follows:

1. Neighborhood Park-School (Elementary). This type of educational-recreation center should be a combination of an elementary school and a neighborhood park. These areas and facilities should be planned for dual use of education and recreation for the people living in a neighborhood. The recommended minimum area for a neighborhood park-school is 20 acres.
2. Community Park-School (Junior High). This type of educational-recreation center should be a combination of a junior high school and community park. These areas and facilities should be planned for dual use of education and recreation for people living in the community. The recommended minimum area for a community park-school is 35 acres.
3. Community Park-School (Senior High). This type of area and facility is planned for the youth and adults in a community to meet a wide range of educational and recreational needs and interests in a community. It is usually referred to as a combination of a community park and high school. The recommended minimum area for a community park-school is 50 acres.[1]

ELEMENTARY SCHOOL

The program of physical education planned for the different age groups in the elementary grades should include certain basic activities that need specific facilities. Children in kindergarten and the first two grades engage in such activities as climbing, hanging, and jumping. Many of their activities should provide for much freedom of movement

[1]*Planning Areas and Facilities for Health, Physical Education and Recreation* (Chicago: The Athletic Institute, 1965), pp. 20–28.

and the development of the large muscles. The program for the third and fourth grades should include running, jumping, kicking, throwing, and catching. The program for the fifth and sixth grades should place a greater emphasis on team games and the development of fundamental skills used in games.

In order to serve the needs and interests of the children from the kindergarten through the sixth grade, the play areas should be close to the building and readily accessible to the elementary classrooms. The elementary physical education and recreation area should have a minimum of 4 acres for 300 pupils and ½ additional acre for each additional 100 pupils.

The kindergarten children should have a section of the elementary-school play area of not less than 5,000 square feet set aside for their use. This area should be separated from the other areas by a fence or hedge and should include: (1) a grassy play area; (2) a small surfaced area; (3) a shaded area; and (4) an apparatus area.

The grassy play area should be level, and free from such safety hazards as rocks and sticks. In this area, children can participate in informal activities and in relatively unorganized games.

The small area of asphalt or all-weather surface, not smaller than a classroom, should be adjacent to the doorway. In this outdoor area, the children can play when the other grassy areas are wet and muddy. It has been found very practical to locate a playhouse adjacent to this surfaced area, to store such equipment as large outdoor blocks, planks, and sawhorses.

The shaded area should be a part of every kindergarten area, for here is where the teacher can do her storytelling. It is very desirable to place in this area such apparatus as climbing structures, horizontal bars, horizontal ladders, and rings. The landing space under all apparatus should be filled with a resilient material such as sand and tanbark, sawdust, or shavings.

Many schools provide separate primary and intermediate-grade play areas. This is very desirable and should be done whenever possible. Both of these play areas should include essentially the same four areas we have just described.

The turf area, for informal and free play and for relatively unorganized games, has to be large enough to include separate areas where the pupils of the fifth and sixth grades can play such games as softball, field ball, line soccer, and other lead-up games.

The asphalt area should be of sufficient size for the same activities that are performed in the gymnasium or playroom. Various markings can be painted on this surfacing, such as different-size circles, hopscotch, shuffleboard courts, and so on. If net games of the lead-up variety are desired, they should be similar to the secondary-school facilities that will be discussed later.

The apparatus area should be so located that it does not break up any large grassy area and, whenever possible, should be a shaded spot. It is desirable to have two separate playground apparatus areas (primary and intermediate), each with the proper size equipment. When selecting apparatus, developmental equipment should be preferred to the recreational type.

SECONDARY SCHOOLS

The program for junior-high school girls should provide a broad foundation in physical education skills upon which can be based the more highly specialized instruction and practice included in the senior-high school program, such as archery, golf, volleyball, tennis, field hockey, speedball, and softball.

The program for junior-high school boys should offer opportunities for instruction and practice in a variety of activities. An intramural program should supplement the instructional program. Some schools have limited competition in certain types of extramural athletics.

The senior-high school girls' and boys' intramural program should include a variety of activities for all pupils, and should be planned so that it can be carried on simultaneously with the interschool activities.

The physical education facilities should be as near the gymnasium and dressing rooms and showers as possible, yet far enough away from the classrooms to prevent playground noise interfering with classroom instruction. Pupils should not have to cross streets, roadways, or driveways when passing from the building to the play areas. The facilities should be accessible to parking areas for the convenience of the community, however.

Four distinct play areas are necessary for good physical education and recreation programs in junior and senior-high schools: (1) courts; (2) high-school girls' area; (3) high-school boys' area; and (4) interschool athletic area.

The Courts Area. The courts should be near the gymnasium and as near the parking facilities as possible. It is desirable to set the net posts in sleeves which are embedded in concrete, so that the posts may be removed and the sleeves capped. This permits the area to be used for many other games and for skating in the winter. Lines of various colors can be painted on the asphalt, a different color for each sport. It is important that the area be fenced. Walls should be erected at one end for handball and the volleying of tennis balls. The area will also provide space for such activities as volleyball, basketball, and badminton. Many schools equip this area with lights so that the recreation program on summer nights can include sports and dancing. The area will also make excellent outdoor teaching stations when the other areas are wet and muddy.

High-School Girls' Area. It is necessary to have a separate area for high-school girls if they are going to have equal opportunities to participate in an adequate physical education program. This space should be located as near the building as possible so that a minimum amount of time is lost going to and from the dressing room and showering room.

The size of the area will depend on the enrollment, but there should be sufficient space for one full-sized official field for such organized games as field hockey, soccer, lacrosse, and softball. There also should be some additional space for the teaching of archery. This should be an isolated area. It is a very important safety precaution to teach archery where there are no pupils who are not participating. If a golf driving range is included in the facilities, the same precautions should be taken.

This area will be used by the girls for class-instruction, and for intramural and interschool activities at other times.

High-School Boys' Area. This area should be separate from the high-school girls' area and the interschool athletic area to avoid scheduling problems. It should be as close as possible to the dressing room and showering room. There should be sufficient space for such activities as softball, soccer, football, speedball, touch football, and lacrosse.

The same principles that apply to the planning of the high-school girls' area hold here.

Interschool Athletic Area. Since this area sometimes holds the community's only athletic facilities, it should be planned for both school and community use. The type of interscholastic program that is offered will determine to a great extent the kind and number of playing areas. If the school is of sufficient size, the following areas should be provided: a football field with a quarter-mile track, a baseball field, a soccer field, a lacrosse field, and several additional practice fields. These areas will also allow for jumping pits, pole-vaulting pits, and so on.

PRINCIPLES IN PLANNING

If the outdoor facilities are going to be functional, then certain basic principles should be used when planning any outdoor areas. Some of these guiding principles are:

☐ Never plan two activities that are played in the same sports season in the same area (e.g., track and baseball are both played in the spring and so should not be in the same location).

☐ Locate such playing areas as soccer fields, football fields, and tennis courts as nearly as possible in a north-south direction, so that the sun will not shine directly in the participants' eyes.

☐ Locate the softball and baseball diamonds in one of the following positions so that the sun does not shine in the participants' eyes: The terrain may determine which of the following settings to use:

The best setting would have the line passing from the pitcher's box to home base form an angle of 20° NE with the long axis that is due north and south.

The second-best setting would have the line passing from the pitcher's box to home base form an angle of 20° SW with the long axis that is due north and south.

The third-best setting would have the line passing from the pitcher's box to home base form an angle of 45° SW with the long axis that is due north and south.

☐ Locate the following areas in the indicated order of proximity to the school building, so that time may be saved throughout the school day:

Instructional area

Intramural area

Interschool area

☐ Locate the outdoor play areas so that pupils do not have to cross any driveways, roadways, or lanes of traffic in order to get to them.

☐ Develop the courts area as a multiple-purpose area in order to save space and money.

☐ Plan for three separate playground areas whenever possible in the elementary grades:

Kindergarten area

Primary area

Intermediate area

facilities: situations and analysis

FIRST SITUATION: LIMITED INDOOR FACILITIES

Mr. Whitney, the director of physical education, has been informed by the superintendent of schools that, until the new building program at the high school has been completed, the indoor physical education facilities will be quite limited. He has asked Mr. Whitney to give him some suggestions as to what type of program can be scheduled during periods of inclement weather.

QUESTIONS

What are considered limited indoor physical education facilities? With limited indoor facilities, what program could be conducted during inclement weather? Should the adjustments in physical education made during the building program be continued after adequate facilities become available?

ANALYSIS

Indoor physical education facilities are considered limited when they can accommodate only a few activities and a minimum number of classes per week. Also limited are the number of activities in the intramural and interscholastic programs and the number of pupils who can participate in them.

During good weather the physical education classes may be held in the outdoor facilities. During inclement weather, use can be made of regular classrooms to teach the knowledge-and-appreciation aspects of physical education. Textbooks, films, and filmstrips may be used to supplement this phase of physical education. Since knowledge is one of the objectives of physical education, such instruction should be continued even after the building program has been completed.

SECOND SITUATION: PLANNING THE COURTS AREA

Mr. Gaffney, the superintendent of schools in Maplewood, has told Mr. Gaines, the director of physical education, that they can plan for

10 tennis courts at the new senior-high school for 1,000 pupils. There is plenty of useable space for these courts, so there is no problem about their location, but Mr. Gaines is wondering whether it would be better to have 10 courts side by side or two rows of 5 courts placed back to back.

QUESTIONS

Are 10 tennis courts adequate? Where should they be located? What direction should they face? Is it more economical to place tennis courts side by side or back to back?

ANALYSIS

Ten tennis courts can accommodate a maximum of 40 pupils participating in a regular game of tennis. For instructional periods and practice of skills, it would be possible to have more pupils participating. For class instruction, 10 courts would be sufficient for a school of 1,000 pupils. Whether they are sufficient for the extra-class program will depend on how extensive the intramural and interschool programs are. Since there is plenty of useable land, there would be no problem about finding space for additional courts at a later date if they were needed.

For supervisory purposes the tennis courts should be located near other playing areas, but still far enough away so that the pupils will not be hit by each other's balls, bats, and other supplies. This means they will be near the school and close to the parking facilities. The tennis courts should be placed in a north-south direction so that the participants are not facing into the sun.

Considerable money could be saved by placing the courts side by side, because they would need less surfacing and fencing. Since there is plenty of space, Mr. Gaines should recommend to Mr. Gaffney that the courts be placed side by side.

**THIRD SITUATION:
GYMNASIUM COURTS**

After the new high-school gymnasium at Harrisville was constructed, the superintendent of schools asked the director of physical education to draw up plans for marking the floor. The director discovered that the gymnasium (100 $\times$ 100 feet) was not quite the right size or shape and that he consequently must choose between a limited number of regulation courts or a sufficient number of less-than-regulation court sizes.

QUESTIONS

Should plans for marking the gymnasium floor be made prior to the construction of the gymnasium? What is the actual size and shape of the gymnasium? What adjustments can be made?

ANALYSIS

All plans for gymnasiums should be based on the program to be conducted in this facility; therefore, all floor markings should have been planned well in advance of the actual construction of the gymnasium.

The actual useable floor space is 100 by 100 feet. It should be noted that every indoors playing area for high-school pupils is rectangular, including courts for basketball, volleyball, badminton, and shuffleboard. It is impossible to put these regulation rectangular courts into a square gymnasium 100 by 100 feet and utilize all the space. It would be better to have a rectangular gymnasium, 84 by 104 feet.

It is possible to reduce the larger courts, such as the basketball and volleyball courts, by a few feet without affecting the actual game. However, a smaller court, such as a badminton court, should not be reduced more than 2 feet in length or 1 foot in width. The minimum recommended safety lanes between courts and between courts and walls should not be reduced.

Teachers who do not want many different colored lines on the floor could put down tape for the courts as they need them. This can be made simple by painting on the floor the right angles at the end lines for each of the courts.

FOURTH SITUATION: DRESSING ROOMS AND SHOWERING ROOMS

As a new director of physical education in Elmhurst Public Schools you are reviewing the proposed building plans for three new elementary schools. You notice that no dressing rooms and showers are proposed for any of the schools. Mr. Bennett, the superintendent of schools, has indicated that they are not being included because the dressing and showering facilities in a school built just two years ago are not being used.

QUESTIONS

At what grade level should dressing and showering be initiated? Why is it important to introduce dressing and showering to pupils in the elementary grades? What type of facilities are needed for carrying on an adequate program of dressing and showering in the elementary grades? Do these facilities have any value for outside groups who may use the school's facilities after school hours? Can you justify not building dressing rooms and showers in new schools because they are not being used in your older schools?

ANALYSIS

It has been found by many elementary schools that a dressing and showering program can be very successfully initiated at the third or fourth-grade level. It is not a problem of getting pupils at these grade levels into the shower, but a problem of getting them out of the shower.

Since it is a desirable health practice to dress properly for physical activities and to shower after physical activity, it is the responsibility of the school to offer the facilities to their pupils. If these health practices are to be inculcated, they should be initiated early, when youngsters are ready. When dressing and showering are introduced in the elementary grades, there are fewer problems with the pupils when they reach the junior and senior-high-school grades, because they have already acquired these desirable health practices.

The only facilities needed are two dressing and showering facilities, one for boys and one for girls. In an elementary school of approximately 600 pupils this would mean four rooms about the same size as four classrooms. Two would be showering rooms equipped with a sufficient number of shower heads, and two would be dressing rooms equipped with an adequate number of lockers. In many communities the elementary schools are used as neighborhood recreation centers for adult recreational and educational programs. With dressing rooms and showers available, a more desirable adult program may be conducted.

It is not justifiable to say that dressing and showering facilities should not be included in a new building program because they are not being used where they already exist. Since it is a desirable health practice to dress and shower, and since the schools have the facilities, it is the responsibility of both the superintendent of schools and the director of physical education to see that this part of the program is implemented. You, as the new director of physical education, should investigate why this has not been done. Is the principal having trouble scheduling time for dressing and showering? Is there a lack of interest on the part of the physical education teachers? After making a thorough investigation, you should have another meeting with Mr. Bennett, to explain the necessity of having dressing rooms and showers in the new schools and of initiating their use where they already exist.

SIXTH SITUATION: PARTITIONING THE GYMNASIUM

The new building program in Oakland last year included a gymnasium in the new high school, with a soundproof folding partition which would create two teaching stations. Because of the rise in the cost of construction it was impossible to put in the partition. It has been suggested that some substitute for the partition, such as a curtain or net, be used.

QUESTIONS

When installing a folding partition in a gymnasium, what are some of the factors to be considered? Can a net or curtain serve as an adequate substitute for the partition?

ANALYSIS

Folding partitions are installed in order to create separate teaching stations in a gymnasium. Therefore, they should be soundproof and extend from the floor to the ceiling. When they are retracted, they should be recessed in a well, so they do not become a hazard. There should be a door in the partition so that one can pass from one teaching station to the other without leaving the gymnasium.

Curtains and nets are poor substitutes for a soundproof folding partition. It would be very difficult to teach different activities in a large gymnasium divided only by curtains or nets, because of the noise. Oakland High School should save its money and not purchase curtains or nets. When monies are available, they should purchase the folding partition.

DISCUSSION NOTES

**PERSONAL PRACTICE-TEACHING EXPERIENCE
RELATED TO TOPIC**

SELECTED REFERENCES

American Association for Health, Physical Education, and Recreation, *Planning Areas and Facilities for Health, Physical Education, and Recreation*. National Education Association, Washington, D.C., 1965.

BISCHOFF, DAVID, "Designed for Participation," *Journal of Health, Physical Education, and Recreation*, XXXVII, (March, 1966), 29–31, 62.

CHAMPLIN, ELLIS, and CASWELL MILES, "Functional Planning and Standards," *Journal of Health, Physical Education, and Recreation*, XXII, (February, 1951), 18–20.

GABRIELSEN, M. ALEXANDER, and CASWELL MILES, *Sports and Recreation Facilities for School and Community*. Englewood Cliffs, N.J.: Prentice-Hall, Inc., 1958.

SCOTT, HARRY, "Facilities for the Future," *Journal of Health, Physical Education, and Recreation*, XXXIII, (April, 1962), 34–36.

SNOWBERGER, CAMPBELL, "A Functional Field House," *Journal of Health, Physical Education, and Recreation*, XXXV, (January, 1964), 38–41, 52.

I GUESS WE SHOULD **CHECK** OUR APPARATUS BEFORE WE PUT IT AWAY
GYMNASIUM

Safety Aspects of Physical Education

CHAPTER 8

Safety is freedom from danger or hazard. Safety entails individual as well as group responsibility and can be achieved only through the continuous efforts of all concerned.

Accidents are events that are not foreseen or expected. They may cause injury, disablement, property damage, loss of time, or even death. When accidents occur, it is quite likely that someone or something has operated ineffectively.

It is essential that maximum precautions be taken to avoid accidents by providing a safe environment for individuals participating in physical education and athletics. Principles which will contribute significantly to the control of accidents are: (1) recognizing hazards; (2) eliminating or reducing hazards; and (3) avoiding additional hazards. When proper precautions are taken, the possibility of negligence will not exist and the chance of a lawsuit will be greatly reduced.

It is the responsibility of the school administration to develop and organize a school-district safety program. Such a program should involve the efforts of all persons affected and reflect sound principles of organization, supervision, and instruction. Specific policies concerning administration, curriculum and instruction, facilities, equipment and supplies, first aid and emergency care, and reporting and investigating accidents should be established. The following policies should serve as guidelines for action.

ADMINISTRATION

☐ A faculty committee, including student representatives, should be organized to advise on safety problems.

☐ Advisory services from outside sources such as physicians, attorneys, insurance, and health and safety specialists should be used in formulating and evaluating accident prevention procedures.

☐ An extensive school safety program for all schools in the district should provide for safety services, safety education and a safe environment.

☐ Specific procedures for reporting and investigating accidents should be established for all schools.

☐ All schools should provide proper insurance protection for students and information concerning coverage should be understood by all concerned.

☐ A detailed plan should exist for handling spectators and crowds at all school activities open to the public.

☐ There should be a plan for the periodic inspection of facilities, equipment, supplies, buildings, and grounds as often as necessary to insure a safe program.

☐ Health histories and medical examinations should be required of students before they participate in physical education class instruction, intramurals, and interschool athletics.

☐ Medical approval should be required for participation in physical education activities following serious illness or injury.

☐ All schools should have specific plans for handling all anticipated emergencies.

CURRICULUM AND INSTRUCTION

☐ In planning the physical education curriculum, activities should be selected which make provision for the given sex, age, ability level, and physical condition of students.

☐ Safety instruction in health and physical education should be an integral part of the curriculum.

☐ Adequate physical-conditioning programs should be provided so students will be prepared to meet the demands of vigorous physical education activities.

☐ Teachers and supervisors of physical education should assist students in realizing the hazards involved in various types of activities.

☐ Close supervision should be provided whenever students participate in hazardous activities.

☐ Teachers should check equipment, supplies and facilities for possible hazards, and teach students to check.
☐ Only teachers qualified to conduct physical education activities should be employed.
☐ Physical and mental differences in students should be considered in the selection and teaching of activities.
☐ Pupils should not be forced to perform physical activities which they obviously feel incapable of performing.
☐ Activities in the curriculum guide should be based upon the age and abilities of pupils and approved by the board of education.
☐ Progression of instruction should be of utmost importance in planning the program of activities.
☐ Organization for instruction should be related to the facilities, equipment, and supplies available, as well as to the type of activity being taught.

FACILITIES

☐ Planning the facilities should be a cooperative effort, involving appropriate school personnel and architects.
☐ New facilities should be laid out without hazards, and designed for future expansion.
☐ The surfacing of the various activity areas should be appropriate for the activities.
☐ Facilities should have proper field or floor markings based on the type of activity and the age levels of the participants.
☐ A color scheme, consistent with recommended safety-color codes, should be used to identify safety devices and hazardous areas or equipment.
☐ Traffic flow in and between facilities, including locker and shower areas, should be planned so as to reduce hazardous situations.
☐ When a hazard in a facility or equipment is identified, it should be corrected immediately or the defective area made inaccessible and its use discontinued until corrective measures have been taken.
☐ Play areas near streets should be fenced.
☐ Activity areas should be level, clean, and free of obstructions.

EQUIPMENT AND SUPPLIES

☐ Selection of equipment and supplies should be based on their contribution to the safety of the participant.

☐ Equipment and supplies should be adapted to environmental conditions, such as weather, sunlight, and topography.

☐ Sufficient area should be provided between equipment to permit safe usage.

☐ Areas adjoining and under playground equipment should have soft, resilient, durable surfaces.

☐ Sufficient equipment and supplies should be available for replacing damaged or worn materials that could create hazards for the participants.

☐ Protective equipment should be required and used when pupils are participating in appropriate physical education activities.

☐ Personal and protective equipment must be properly fitted to provide participants with maximum safety.

☐ Hazardous equipment and supplies such as apparatus, trampolines, and bows and arrows should be properly stored and secured.

FIRST AID AND EMERGENCY CARE

☐ Persons teaching physical education activities should be competent in administering first aid.

☐ All members of the faculty should receive formal instruction in first aid and periodic refresher courses as often as necessary to maintain the competence necessary for providing emergency assistance.

☐ The school physician should determine medical eligibility to participate in physical education activities.

☐ A physician should be in attendance at all interscholastic contests where the activity involves contact. He should be readily available during practice sessions for such activities.

☐ The health record of each student should contain information about contacting parents or guardians, as well as the name of the family physician and the preferred hospital.

☐ The staff should be informed about any health condition that might cause an emergency when the pupil is participating in school activities.

☐ Students should receive first-aid instruction appropriate to their learning level.

REPORTING AND INVESTIGATING ACCIDENTS

☐ All schools of a district should participate in a standardized procedure of accident reporting, using a uniform report form.

SAFETY ASPECTS OF PHYSICAL EDUCATION   127

☐ Detailed information should be recorded about all injuries, however slight.

☐ The appropriate administrative officers should be notified immediately of all severe accidents.

☐ All accident reports pertaining to physical education should be examined by the director of physical education and other appropriate personnel.

☐ All accident reports should become a part of the student's permanent health record.

☐ Accident reports should be analyzed and summarized, and recommendations should be made by the director of physical education to the administration and board of education.

safety: situations and analysis

**FIRST SITUATION:
SAFE PLAYGROUND EQUIPMENT**

Mr. Farley, the physical education teacher at Elm Street Elementary School, has been informed by Mr. Hart, the principal, that the P.T.A. is going to give the school money for some playground apparatus. Mr. Hart wants Mr. Farley to give him a list of apparatus that is considered safe and worthwhile for elementary-grade pupils.

QUESTIONS

What are some of the different types of playground apparatus? What is some safe elementary-school playground apparatus? Why should elementary schools purchase playground equipment? What type of surfacing should be underneath playground apparatus?

ANALYSIS

Generally speaking there are three different types of playground apparatus: (1) recreational, such as swings, slides, and teeters; (2) developmental, such as jungle gyms, hanging bars, and hanging ladders; and (3) creative-imaginative, including some recreation and some developmental. Many of the last type take fantastic forms, including animals and trees.

It has been found that most present-day playground apparatus is safe. The one piece of equipment apparatus that has been found to be unsafe is the giant stride (a pole with attached chain and ring). Most schools have either removed it or adjusted it to be used for tether ball.

It is natural for elementary-school children to climb and hang. In order to meet this natural urge, elementary schools must provide opportunities for their pupils to use developmental apparatus. Such equipment contributes to physical fitness through the development of strength, endurance, and agility.

Many pupils are interested in using recreational apparatus during their leisure time, and the school should meet the interests of its pupils by providing this type of equipment.

The surfacing under playground apparatus should be a resilient type, such as sawdust, sand, or a mixture of sand and tanbark.

SECOND SITUATION:
AN INDOOR RELAY RACE

Mr. Fredericks, the supervisor of physical education, has observed an elementary-classroom teacher teaching her first-grade pupils to run a relay race. The pupils run to the end of the gymnasium, touch the wall, and return to the starting line. Mr. Fredericks should make several suggestions to this teacher.

QUESTIONS

Should gymnasium walls be used for turning points in relay races? What should be used for turning markers in relay races? What safety factors should be considered in conducting relay races?

ANALYSIS

Mr. Fredericks should inform the classroom teacher that the walls of the gymnasium should not be used as turning points during relay races because serious injuries may occur. Many serious accidents have been recorded, even when the walls have been padded.

There are many safe turning markers, including Indian clubs, plastic bowling pins, and traffic safety markers. These should be placed far enough away from the wall so there is no safety hazard.

The following safety precautions should be taken when conducting a relay race.

The teacher should explain the rules and directions very carefully.

All pupils should run the same pattern.

All pupils should stay in line and be a safe distance behind the finish line.

All pupils should be wearing sneakers. They should not be allowed to run wearing just socks.

The gymnasium floor must be free of dirt and debris.

THIRD SITUATION: SIMULTANEOUS ACTIVITIES

Miss Brown, a new physical education teacher at Milford High School, has a class of eighth-grade pupils in a gymnastics unit. She has set up the uneven parallel bars, trampoline, balance beam, and side horse with six girls at each piece of equipment. All of the activities are going on simultaneously.

QUESTIONS

How many pieces of apparatus can a physical education teacher adequately supervise? To what extent should pupil-leaders be used in gymnastics? What safety factors should be considered when using apparatus?

ANALYSIS

Miss Brown, being a beginning teacher with limited experience, should not teach with more than one piece of apparatus at a time unless she has assistance from another teacher. More than one pice of apparatus can be used if the pupils have had considerable experience in gymnastics, and if a highly trained pupil-leader is available for each piece of equipment.

The several safety factors that should be considered when teaching gymnasium apparatus are:

Carefully inspect the apparatus every day to see that it is in safe condition.

Make sure that the mats are fixed and in proper position.

Make sure that apparatus such as the horse and the parallel bars are fixed so that they do not move when mounted.

When an advanced stunt is to be performed, make sure that there are mature spotters who are properly positioned.

Stunts should be performed in a series of progressions.

FOURTH SITUATION:
SNEAKERS

Mrs. Garvey, the physical education teacher in Monticello Elementary School, has several pupils in her primary-grade classes who do not have sneakers. She wants them to participate in the classes, so has asked them to remove their shoes and join the class on the gymnasium floor.

QUESTIONS

Should children in the primary grades who do not have sneakers be allowed to participate in activities in the gymnasium when they remove their shoes? Should the teacher insist that all pupils have sneakers when participating? Should shoes with rubber soles be used as a substitute for sneakers?

ANALYSIS

Children who do not wear sneakers should not be allowed to participate in physical education classes in the gymnasium in their socks. Many teachers will ask the children to remove their shoes and participate, but if one of these children is injured the teacher could be held negligent. Negligence exists when a person does something which a reasonably prudent person should know or would know might lead to injury. Negligence also exists when a person omits doing something which might prevent an injury. In this case, Mrs. Garvey may be proven negligent because a reasonably prudent person would know that running on the gymnasium floor in socks is dangerous, and she permitted it.

Teachers should insist that all pupils participating in physical education be appropriately dressed, including the wearing of sneakers. The teacher who does not insist has, in essence, omitted doing something which might prevent an injury. Some schools keep extra pairs of sneakers of assorted sizes which pupils may borrow when they forget their own.

Shoes with rubber soles are not an adequate substitute. Pupils using this type of footwear in the gymnasium seem to have problems with turned ankles. Moreover, many accidents have occurred in kicking games when shoes have been worn in place of sneakers.

**FIFTH SITUATION:
GYMNASIUM FLOORING**

A new elementary school is being planned in Belmont. The principal, who is economy-minded, has indicated to the superintendent that it would cost less money to place tile directly over concrete in the gymnasium. What should be the reaction of the physical education teacher to this suggestion?

QUESTIONS

Is it desirable to use tile over concrete for flooring in a gymnasium? What materials are desirable for gymnasium floors?

ANALYSIS

It is not desirable for a gymnasium floor to be constructed with tile over concrete because of the lack of resiliency. This not only creates a hazard to falling youngsters but is a very fatiguing surface for the teacher who must stand, walk, and run on it all day.

A gymnasium floor should have an even resiliency but still maintain a firmness that will give a lively rebound to a bouncing ball. This resiliency is important for safety, and also for the prevention of foot, leg, and back fatigue. Wooden floors of maple, birch, or beech seem to be the most desirable. Tiles and other synthetic materials may also be used satisfactorily, if they are not placed directly on top of concrete.

**SIXTH SITUATION:
PLAYING FOOTBALL WITH A HANDICAP**

The parents of a boy in Summerville High School would like their son, who has only one eye, to play varsity football. The school has a policy that such handicapped pupils cannot play contact sports. The family physician has indicated that it is permissible for the boy to play.

QUESTIONS

Should handicapped pupils be allowed to participate in interscholastic sports? Is the school's policy a desirable one?

ANALYSIS

Some handicapped pupils may participate in certain interscholastic sports without permanent damage to their health and well-being. The physician has to weigh very carefully his decision about whether a pupil should participate in interscholastic sports, especially contact sports, if he has a physical defect.

Some athletes with handicaps such as asthma and diabetes have participated in sports for years without any damage to their health. If a pupil is blind in one eye, however, the hazards are too great to let him participate in sports involving body contact. If the good eye were injured, total blindness might be the end result.

The school's policy is a good one because the chances are too great to take. The personnel should try to get the boy interested in other non-contact fall sports, such as cross-country running. When pupils have handicaps such as one eye, one kidney, or a defective heart, it is probably good school policy to have the medical recommendation of the specialist in each case. If the school district has a physician, then he should make the final medical decision about whether a handicapped pupil should play interscholastic sports. Since the team represents the school, the school physician should have the final say when there is a difference of medical opinion.

DISCUSSION NOTES

**PERSONAL PRACTICE TEACHING EXPERIENCE
RELATED TO TOPIC**

SELECTED REFERENCES

American Association for Health, Physical Education and Recreation, *School Safety Policies*. National Education Association, Washington, D.C., 1968.

———, *The Physical Education Instructor and Safety*. Washington, D.C.: National Education Association, 1948.

CURTIS, PAUL, *Safety and Fun Synonymous*. Chicago: National Safety Council, 1955.

FLORIO, A. E., and G. T. STAFFORD, *Safety Education*. New York: McGraw-Hill Book Company, 1962.

STACK, HERBERT J., and J. DUKE ELKOW, *Education for Safe Living*. Englewood Cliffs, N.J.: Prentice-Hall, Inc., 1966.

STRASSER, MARLAND K., JAMES E. AARON, RALPH C. BOHN, and JOHN R. EALES, *Fundamentals of Safety Education,* New York: The Macmillan Company, 1964.

Legal Aspects   CHAPTER 9

of

Physical Education

The program of physical education is of such a nature that teachers and administrators are frequently placed in situations where liability may occur. Therefore, they should be conversant with the law as it relates to their function and they should conduct their program properly, so that negligence can be avoided.

LAWS, REGULATIONS, AND POLICIES

Public education is a function of the state, but the responsibilty of educating pupils is that of the local boards of education. Powers given to these representatives of local government are stated in *laws* that have been passed by state legislatures. In addition to these laws, state education departments often have established *regulations* to assist local school districts in carrying out their function of educating pupils. Although these regulations are not law, they may carry as much authority as law. In addition to state laws and regulations, school districts establish *policies* to facilitate the administration of their schools.

When problems arise between individuals or groups, the matter may be taken to court. It is here that *attorneys* give their *opinions* on the legal interpretations, but it is the *court* that renders the *decision*. The decision of the court establishes a precedent for similar cases that may follow, unless the state legislature passes new or revised laws on the subject.

WHO PAYS FOR ACCIDENTS

The education laws of the various states require that all pupils attend school. These same laws, in most states, require that these same pupils take physical education whether they want to or not. The school provides physical education facilities that the student must use, be they desirable or undesirable. He also is exposed to various pieces of equipment and supplies. The competence of his teacher and the adequacy of supervision cannot be questioned by the pupil.

Suppose the pupil is injured. The question of who is at fault then arises. Was there negligence on the part of the pupil, the teacher, the school district, or another pupil? There are expenses, the doctor, hospital, nurses, and drugs. Who pays for all this—the child, the teacher, or the school board? This question is decided in the courts. In almost every aspect of the operation of a school, the educator is recognized as the highly trained expert whose professional know-how gives him the special qualifications to handle school problems. However, when an accident to a pupil is involved, the school, with its administrators and teachers, is not looked upon in the same light. This is the one time that the school must measure up to the standards of the lay person, to the judgment of the citizens of a community. A liability suit places the teacher and the school district in a court where the decision will be made by a jury of laymen. The question of who is at fault will not be decided by professional educators, but by a jury of citizens.

COMMON TERMS USED

Action. The ordinary proceeding in a court of justice by which one person seeks the enforcement or protection of a right, or the redress or prevention of a wrong.

Accident. An event that occurs without one's foresight or expectation.

Defendant. The person being sued or the person against whom court action is brought.

Liability. A condition which gives rise to an obligation and a responsibility to do a particular thing to be enforced by court action.

Negligence. The failure to act as a reasonably prudent person would act under the particular circumstances.

Plaintiff. The person who brings suit for the purpose of seeking a remedy for an injury to his rights.

Tort. A legal wrong for which damages may be obtained by court action.

Vis major. An act of God, a situation in which the defendant had no control over the accident.

REQUIREMENTS FOR AN ACTION IN NEGLIGENCE

When there is an accident, the plaintiff must allege that there was injury to himself or his property; that the defendant was negligent; and that he, the plaintiff, did not contribute to the injury.

In the nature of the relationship, the school and its personnel have the legal responsibility of exercising care to prevent injuries to their pupils. Negligence results when there is a breach of this duty. Negligence is a failure to act as a reasonably prudent person would act under the particular circumstances.

Negligence can consist of an omission as well as an action. If a person fails to do something expected of him by the law, he can be negligent. Also, doing something contrary to what the law expects can be negligence.

A reasonably prudent person is a mythical person established by law. His major characteristic is foresight. If a reasonable man of ordinary prudence should have foreseen the harmful consequences of the behavior, then there is negligence—failure to avoid trouble that reasonably could or should have been foreseen or anticipated.

When there is a liability suit, the critical question that is answered is: Should or could the teacher, in the exercise of reasonable prudence and foresight, have anticipated danger or hurt to a pupil under the particular circumstances? If the answer is "Yes," then the teacher is negligent if he failed to act so as to prevent such foreseeable danger and harm.

The specific facts in each case are all-important in determining negligence. What may be prudent with high-school pupils may not be prudent with elementary-grade pupils. The physical education teacher assigned to a playground may be prudent, but the principal who failed to assign enough teachers to the supervision of that playground may have been highly imprudent.

Even when negligence exists, there are some cases where there is no liability because of certain legal defenses. This occurs when the injury was due to the pupil's own contributory negligence and when the injury was due to an "act of God."

COMMON AREAS OF NEGLIGENCE

☐ Poor selection of activities. Failure to recognize different degrees of caution to be used in respect to the limitations of pupils due to skill, age, and sex.

☐ The absence of protective measures. Failure to see the dangers involved in certain situations.

☐ Unsafe condition of buildings, grounds, equipment and supplies. Failure to inspect physical education facilities and equipment at regular intervals, allowing pupils to use faulty apparatus or failing to control the pupil's use of areas, equipment, and supplies.

☐ Inadequate supervision. Failure to provide a sufficient number of qualified supervisors for all play activities.

☐ Unreasonable risks. Failure to prevent pupils from taking unreasonable risks.

☐ Inadequate control measures. Failure to make necessary corrections, so that the actions of others within or outside a class might create a hazardous situation.

☐ Poor judgment. Failure of a teacher to use common sense, so that his actions increase the risks of harm or injury.

☐ Undesirable health practices. Failure to administer proper first aid; exceeding the limitations of first aid by giving treatment.

☐ Unauthorized transportation. Failure to use a sanctioned means of transportation.

DEFENSES AGAINST NEGLIGENCE

☐ Act of God. A condition which is beyond the control of any human being, such as a sudden storm. If prudent action still could have prevented the injury, this is not a defense.

☐ Sudden emergency. For example, a physical education teacher, when teaching swimming, rushes to aid one of his pupils who is in danger of drowning. He bumps into one of his other students and injures him. The court may well rule in favor of the teacher, whose immediate objective was the saving of a pupil's life.

☐ Contributory negligence by the pupil. When a person participates in certain physical education activities, he accepts the fact that certain risks are inherent and that accidents may occur despite safeguards and precautions.

LEGALITY OF WAIVER AND PERMISSION SLIPS

A waiver is an agreement in which a person forgoes certain of his rights. When a parent signs a waiver, he can only waive his own right to sue as a parent. He cannot waive the right of the pupil to sue as an individual. Litigation has sometimes been avoided by parental ignorance of this fact.

A permission slip is a document signed by a parent authorizing the pupil to participate in an activity. The only legal value such a form has is that it shows that the school uses reasonable care with pupils and that the parent has received notice of his child's participation in the activity.

SCHOOL DISTRICT LIABILITY

In American Law, the normal rule of *respondent superior* is that an employer is liable for the negligence of his employees during the course of their employment. This is not true for most school boards in the United States, however. The reason lies in our past history. When the United States won its freedom from England, our state and national governments succeeded to the legal status of the King of England, and "The King can do no wrong."

Today, about two centuries later, the rule of governmental immunity still prevails in most of our states. In the performance of its governmental functions, the state, or the school district, cannot be held liable for negligence. The school board cannot legally purchase liability insurance without statutory authority, because a school board cannot spend public monies to insure itself against a nonexistent liability.

Thus, the general rule of governmental immunity protects a school district from liability for negligence in the absence of specific statutes to the contrary. Because this doctrine has been unfair, however, some states have created statutory exceptions to the rule in one form or another. The three states of New York, New Jersey, and Connecticut have mandatory statutes which say that if teachers are held liable for negligence as a result of an accident connected with their school duties, the school district will "save them harmless," or pay the judgment against them. The states of Wyoming, Oregon, and Massachusetts have permissive laws to the same effect, authorizing but not requiring the states to pay the liability judgment against the teacher.

legal aspects: situations and analysis

FIRST SITUATION: BOXING

Mr. Brown, the physical education teacher at Brownville High School has two boys in his fifth-period class who are misbehaving. He has the two boys stay after school and, as a disciplinary measure, has them box three rounds. Although he gives no instruction in boxing during physical education class, he thinks this is a good way of punishing boys.

QUESTIONS

Is boxing a desirable activity to be taught in physical education classes? Is this a desirable means of disciplining pupils? What is adequate instruction in physical education activities?

ANALYSIS

Boxing is not a desirable activity to be taught in physical education classes because the objectives of boxing are contrary to the objectives of physical education. The primary aim of boxing is injury to the opponent. The American Association for Health, Physical Education and Recreation, and the Society of State Directors of Health, Physical Education and Recreation, have both passed resolutions condemning boxing as an undesirable interscholastic athletic activity. Since boxing is regarded as unsuitable because of the potential danger, boxing should not be taught.

Since boxing is not a desirable activity for pupils, it should not be used as a means of discipline. It is questionable whether a teacher should use any physical education activity as a means of discipline. If such a procedure is followed, the teacher should make sure that adequate instruction has been provided and that practice by the pupils has preceded actual participation in the activity. In several cases, physical education teachers have been found liable for injuries that occurred to pupils who attempted to do an exercise beyond their skill. In one case, in New York, it was held that the lack of instruction before requiring a pupil to do a somersault may constitute negligence.[1] Two other cases were boxing and a head-stand exercise.[2] These activities were found inherently dangerous by the courts. Moreover, the evidence showed that the previous instruction had been inadequate and that the pupils had not been warned of the dangers.

Adequate instruction in physical education activities means the teaching of skills through the progression of instruction. There must be adequate time for pupils to practice these skills. The teacher should be a qualified and certified person. Every time a school district finds itself

---

[1] *Goval* v *Board of Education of Albany*, 60 N.E. (2d) 133 (New York, 1944).
[2] *LaValley* v *Stanford*, 70 N.Y.S. (2d) 460 (New York, 1947); *Gardner* v *State of New York*, 22 N.E. (2d) 344 (New York, 1939).

in a lawsuit because of negligence, the first question which must be answered is the competency of the person who had charge of the children at the time the accident happened. If a person holds a teaching license, such license is prima facie evidence of competency.

SECOND SITUATION: A CROWDED GYMNASIUM

The gymnasium in Jordan High School is only 43 by 74 feet, and it has two basketball courts and six baskets. The second-period physical education class has 60 pupils. Mr. Browning, the physical education teacher, has asked the principal to schedule smaller classes.

QUESTIONS

What are adequate facilities? What constitutes inadequate supervision? What are the legal implications?

ANALYSIS

Physical education facilities are considered adequate when they can accommodate all of the activities for all of the pupils on a daily basis, including class instruction, intramurals, and interscholastics.

Inadequate supervision is failure to conform to the supervisory standards usually expected of one who is in charge of a group of persons engaged in physical education activities. Court cases most often involve teachers absenting themselves from a place they are supervising.[3]

In cases of litigation involving supervision, the facts are vital. There are no absolute rules about the number of pupils that should be assigned to a teacher or supervisor. However, there have been cases of inadequate supervision where one teacher was assigned the sole responsibility for supervising a large number of pupils.[4]

The principal of Jordan High School should schedule smaller classes because the gymnasium is inadequate for such a large number of pupils. This was made evident in the court case of a school district with a gymnasium 80 by 43 feet, with eight overlapping basketball courts. All eight courts were used simultaneously. One of the participants was hurt. The court held this to be negligence because the school

---

[3] *Ohman v Board of Education of New York City,* 90 N.E. (2d) 474 (New York, 1949).
[4] *Charonnat v San Francisco Unified School District,* 133 P. (2d) 643 (California, 1943); *Forgnone v Salvatore Union Elementary School District,* 106 P. (2d) 932 (California, 1940).

should have anticipated injury in so overcrowded a gymnasium when a strenuous game requiring movement was being played.[5]

THIRD SITUATION:
DIFFICULT GYMNASTICS

At Meridian High School, Mr. Scott, the physical education teacher, teaches a unit in gymnastics. One of the students, Tom Jones, who is obese, is having a difficult time doing very simple stunts. On Tuesday, Mr. Scott has the boys doing a running dive over four boys who are kneeling on the mat. Tom says he can't perform the stunt, but Mr. Scott insists that he try. Tom makes the attempt and breaks his arm.

QUESTIONS

Should every pupil be made to perform every activity in a physical education class? What adjustments should the teacher make for individual differences?

ANALYSIS

Every pupil should not be expected to perform every activity. Failure to exercise varying degrees of caution as dictated by such factors as age, skill, and sex can be negligence. Teachers should be required to select and conduct activities appropriate to the physical and mental abilities of the participants.

The physical education teacher should know the physical and mental limitations of each pupil, and how they are reflected in performance. The basis for his information is the annual health examination, which is most effectively used in school districts where there is close cooperation between the health-service personnel and the physical education staff.

FOURTH SITUATION:
UNIFORMS

The policy in Hanes High School is to have all pupils dress in a physical education uniform. Mrs. Jenkins has told Mrs. Green, the girls' physical education teacher, that her daughter was not going to get

[5]*Bauer* v *Board of Education*, 285 Appellate Division 1148, 140 New York, Supp. 2d 167 (1955).

dressed in a uniform for physical education. She also indicated that the school could not make her daughter wear such a uniform.

QUESTIONS

Can a school district require that a pupil wear a prescribed uniform for physical education activities? What are desirable uniforms? Should the physical education teacher wear a teaching uniform?

ANALYSIS

Generally speaking, a school district cannot prescribe the type of dress a pupil may wear to school. There are exceptions, however, and one of these is related to safety. Since the type of clothing worn during physical education activities can affect a pupil's safety, a school district can mandate that a pupil wear proper dress in physical education classes. However, the school district cannot insist that this uniform be a particular color.

It is nice to have all pupils dressed alike, but there is no legal requirement by which a board of education can make all pupils wear the same color uniform. Teachers should attempt to motivate pupils to purchase the standard uniform because it establishes group identity and contributes to school morale. The attire does not have to be elaborate. The girls' uniform can be plain, washable shorts and blouse, or a one-piece suit plus a sweatshirt. For boys, a cotton T-shirt, shorts, sweatshirt and sweat pants are desirable. Both boys and girls should wear suitable footwear. For special activities such as swimming, appropriate uniforms should be worn. All pupils should be taught to keep their uniforms neat, clean, and attractive in appearance, and the teacher should make every effort to see that health standards are met by all pupils.

Since physical education teachers should set the proper example for the pupils to follow, they should wear appropriate uniforms when teaching physical education. Such leadership will help to inspire pupils to dress properly for all activities.

DEFECTIVE PLAYGROUND EQUIPMENT
FIFTH SITUATION:

Mr. Jacobs, the supervisor of physical education for the Fairview Public Schools, has the responsibility for seeing that all playground apparatus is in a safe condition. He notices that a 12-foot slide on the

Grant Street Elementary School playground is in need of repair. What action should Mr. Jacobs take?

QUESTIONS

What steps should Mr. Jacobs take to repair the slide? Would there be negligence involved if an accident occurred on the slide before the situation was corrected?

ANALYSIS

Since Mr. Jacobs is responsible for seeing that all playground apparatus is in safe condition, he should order the removal of the entire slide at once. He should also immediately notify the principal and all teachers at the Grant Street Elementary School that no pupil should be allowed to use the slide in its present, unsafe condition. Prior to the removal of the slide, steps should be taken to make sure that it is impossible for any person to use it. One preventive measure that should be taken is the sealing off of the stairway to the slide by securing boards across the width of the stairs on front and back. Unless preventive measures are taken, there is probable negligence on the part of the school district and Mr. Jacobs.

There have been court cases where school districts have been held liable for unsafe playground apparatus. In one case, involving a pupil injured on a defective slide on a playground, the school district was held liable.[6] In another case involving a defective slide, the school district was held liable for maintaining unsafe conditions on a playground.[7]

SIXTH SITUATION:
WRESTLING COMPETITION

Mr. Groves, the physical education teacher, is teaching a unit in wrestling at Hudson High School. The boys have all been given adequate instruction in the various techniques of wrestling. Since they are now ready for competitive wrestling, he has asked the boys to choose their wrestling partners.

QUESTIONS

Is it good practice for pupils to select their own partners for physical education activities? What procedures should Mr. Groves have followed in selecting partners for a wrestling competition?

[6]*Howell* v *Union Free School District No. 1*, 194 N.Y.S. 333 (New York, 1937).
[7]*Lemak* v *City of Pittsburgh*, 23A (2d) 354, (Pennsylvania, 1941).

ANALYSIS

Where there is no body contact and where such factors as height and weight have little effect on the activity, it may be desirable to permit pupils to select their own partners. This would apply to such activities as tennis, golf, table tennis, and bowling. In activities where the mismatching of pupils could create a safety hazard, however, the physical education teacher should make sure that pupils are properly matched. For example, for an activity such as soccer, the teacher should consider such factors as proficiency, height, and weight. Mr. Groves should attempt to match the boys on the basis of weight, strength, and also wrestling skill, since all of these are significant factors in wrestling.

In a related court case, involving a mismatching of heights and weights in a supervised soccer game, the court found negligence because of failure to assure proper matching. One pupil was kicked in the head by another and suffered serious injury.[8] In another case, where such factors had been considered in selecting wrestling partners, the court found no negligence. Here the activity was under the supervision of a competent person who had approved the matching of two boys after comparison of weights and after watching them wrestle.[9]

[8]*Brooks* v *Board of Education*, 29 misc. 2d (New York) 19, 205 New York Supp. 2d 777 (1960), aff'd 15 App. Div. 2d 495, 222 New York Supp. 2d 184 (1961), aff'd 12 New York, 2d 971, 189 N.E. 2d 497 (1963).

[9]*Vendrell* v *School District*, 226 Oregon 263, 360 F. 2d 282, 288 (1961).

DISCUSSION NOTES

**PERSONAL PRACTICE-TEACHING EXPERIENCE
RELATED TO TOPIC**

SELECTED REFERENCES

DYER, D. B., and J. G. LICHTIG, *Liability in Public Recreation.* Milwaukee: C. C. Nelson Publishing Company, 1949.

GARBER, L. O., *Tort and Contractual Liability of School Districts.* Danville, Ill.: Interstate Printers and Publishers, Inc., 1963.

HAMILTON, R. R., *School Liability.* Chicago: National Safety Council, 1952.

LEIBEE, HOWARD C., *Liability for Accidents in Physical Education, Athletics, Recreation.* Ann Arbor, Mich.: Ann Arbor Publishers, 1952.

ROSENFIELD, HARRY N., *Liability for School Accidents.* New York: Harper & Row Publishers, Incorporated, 1940.

MISS SNYDER, HOW CAN ANYONE FLUNK PHYSICAL EDUCATION?
REPORT CARD
PHYSICAL EDUCATION: MISS SNYDER

Evaluation CHAPTER 10

Evaluation is becoming more recognized as a necessary and integral part of the physical education program. There is an increasing awareness that in order to demonstrate the benefits of a physical education program and in order to conduct it in the most efficient way, measurement and evaluation are necessary.

Measurement and evaluation are highly related, but they are not equivalent. Evaluation is broader than measurement. Measurement merely indicates status by answering such questions as how much, how often, and how many; evaluation on the other hand, goes beyond the pure mechanics of testing and measuring. It is an appraisal of the results of measurement in terms of aims and objectives, and it is important that evaluation include a follow-up. As a consequence of evaluation, objectives may be changed, programs revised, facilities improved, staff increased and methodology changed—all to create a better teaching and learning situation for the pupil. In order for evaluation to be successful, however, it must be continuous. Both the product (pupil) and the process (program) have to be measured frequently.

There are still some physical educators who doubt that educational outcomes can be evaluated. This misconception has existed among educators for many years. It was about a half-century ago that, because of this attitude, Edward Lee Thorndike made his famous statement that whatever exists at all exists in amounts and that anything that exists in amounts can be measured.

Not all measurement in physical education is objective. Much of it is not as simple as the tests which give results in terms of inches, feet, seconds, and minutes. There are some characteristics which are impossible to measure objectively; consequently, results cannot be expressed in quantitative terms and the measurement is subjective and frequently less reliable than objectively determined results. The challenge to physical educators is to make such measurements as objective and systematic as possible, so that they will have greater reliability. Qualities and factors that are not readily isolated or identified are difficult to measure and can only be expressed in qualitative terms.

THE PURPOSES OF MEASUREMENT AND EVALUATION

The function of measurement in the school today must keep pace with our changing philosophy of education. Modern education demands that each child be given the opportunity to progress as rapidly as he can or as slowly as he must. Physical education is a continuous process in which, with skillful teaching, the development of the child is guided on the basis of the speed, direction, and extent of his previous growth. If the maximum growth and development of each child is to be the main goal of our physical education program, then frequent measures of each child's physical fitness, skills, knowledge, and social competence must be made. The primary purpose of measurement and evaluation is to assess status, and thus identify progress or achievement.

Some of the secondary uses of measurement devices and evaluation techniques are:

- ☐ To classify pupils.
- ☐ To use in counseling pupils.
- ☐ To motivate pupils.
- ☐ To contribute to research.
- ☐ To use for marking purposes.

TYPES OF MEASURING INSTRUMENTS

There are several devices available for the evaluation of physical education. All are useful, but some are more popular than others:

Observation. Observation is a very good technique if the teacher knows what to look for. Such instruments as score cards and rating scales can make observations more objective.

Check Lists. A simple list of important items to look for when engaged in appraising pupils makes for more objective and worthwhile evaluation.

Interviews. An effective measuring device which can be quite effective in determining how pupils feel about various parts of the physical education program.

Records. Cumulative records are a necessity if the teacher is to determine the pupil's status and progress.

Tests. These are the most common means of appraising the pupil's status and progress. They should include tests of physical fitness, knowledge, and skills.

THE SELECTION OF APPROPRIATE TESTS

Standardized tests should not be administered merely because testing is the current educational fad. Nor should a test be administered simply because it is a good test: It should be good for a specific purpose. Appropriate tests must be chosen if best use is to be made of the results. The choices should be made in the light of the objectives sought.

CRITERIA FOR SELECTION OF TESTS

In order for the physical education teacher to judge whether some tests are better than others, standards are needed. Some of the criteria of good tests that are generally accepted are:

Validity. Does the test measure what it is suppose to measure? Does it tell the truth?

Reliability. Is the test consistent? Will the same results occur when the test is repeated by the same group under like conditions with the same teacher?

Objectivity. The degree of agreement among persons scoring the same test. Will the same scores result when the test is repeated by the same group under like conditions with different teachers?

Norms. A norm is the average performance on a test of pupils of a certain age or in a certain grade. Norms facilitate comparisons and interpretations. It must be remembered that in any normal group of pupils, half of the group may be expected to be below the norm, or average.

Economy. Test equipment and supplies should be readily available and inexpensive. The test should take a minimum amount of time. The results should be readily usable.

COMPETENCIES NEEDED IN EVALUATION

Evaluations must be made by qualified personnel if they are to be effective. There are certain competencies that both beginning and experienced teachers must have in order to conduct a desirable program of measurement. Barrow and McGee have indicated that a physical education teacher must be competent in the following area:

Knowledge of Where to Locate Tests (Availability). First, the teacher must know what measurement instruments are available and where the information for their effective use may be found.

Knowledge of How to Evaluate Tests (Evaluation). Second, the teacher must know how to properly evaluate the tests which are being used.

Knowledge of How to Administer Tests (Administration). Third, when the appropriate instrument has been selected, the teacher must be able to administer the measurement program so that the resulting data will be valid and reliable and so that there is no waste of valuable time.

Knowledge of How to Interpret Test Results (Interpretation). Fourth, the teacher must be able to interpret what test scores mean when they are obtained.

Knowledge of How to Use Test Results (Use). Fifth, the teacher must have knowledge of the use that can be made of measurement results so that the effectiveness of the program can be improved.

Knowledge of How to Construct Written and Motor Performance Tests (Test Construction). Sixth, the teacher should be able to construct scientifically teacher-made tests.

Knowledge of How to Use Elementary Statistics (Statistics). Seventh, in order to interpret test results, to develop norms, and to construct homemade tests, the teacher must know how to use elementary statistics.

Knowledge of How Evaluation Relates to the Total Program (Program). Eighth, the teacher must be able to see the relationship between evaluation and the physical education program.[1]

evaluation:
situations and analysis

**FIRST SITUATION:
CRITERIA FOR MARKS**

Mr. Lyons, the director of health and physical education, has been told by the superintendent of schools that the board of education is

[1] Harold M. Barrow and Rosemary McGee, *A Practical Approach to Measurement in Physical Education* (Philadelphia: Lea & Febiger, 1964), pp. 28–30.

willing to grant credit for high-school physical education if the staff can show them a sound working system. At present, the only test administered to the classes is the AAHPER Fitness Test.

QUESTIONS

What objectives of physical education should the marking system be based upon? What weight should be given to each objective in figuring the final mark? Are there standardized tests to measure a pupil's status and progress in physical education? Should a mark be given in physical education even though credit is not granted?

ANALYSIS

Physical education marks should be based upon the recognized objectives of physical education, including physical fitness, skills, knowledge, and social competence. The weight given each objective should reflect the philosophy of the physical education staff. Therefore, Mr. Lyons should discuss with his staff what objectives should be considered and what weight should be given to each one.

There are some standardized tests for the measurement of the physical fitness, skills, and knowledge of high-school students. There are also ways of measuring social competence, including sociometric techniques. In order to have a sound marking system, the tests administered should be appropriate for all objectives, not just physical fitness.

Marks are given in other subjects. In order for physical education to be recognized as part of the total educational curriculum, marks should be given in physical education whether credit is granted or not.

SECOND SITUATION: EVALUATING MANY PUPILS

Mr. Jenkins is the only physical education teacher in the two elementary schools in Brownsville. He teaches all pupils in grades 1 to 6 in each school, which means he teaches approximately 1,200 different pupils every week. He has been asked by the elementary-school principal to make an evaluation of each pupil's progress in physical education.

QUESTIONS

How is a pupil's status and progress in physical education determined? Can a person who teaches 1,200 different pupils every week evaluate them adequately? Are there measuring instruments adequate for determining a pupil's status and progress in physical education at the elementary-grade level? Should the elementary-classroom teacher also be involved in evaluating the pupils physical education?

ANALYSIS

The evaluation of a pupil's status and progress in physical education should be based upon the recognized objectives of physical education, such as physical fitness, skills, knowledge, and social competence.

It would not be possible for Mr. Jenkins to make an adequate evaluation of 1,200 pupils. In fact, it would be almost impossible for a teacher even to know the names of 1,200 different pupils when he teaches them only once a week.

Some standardized tests are available for measuring the physical fitness of intermediate-grade pupils. Like other teachers, the physical educator must use teacher-made tests to measure skills and knowledge. In addition, he must subjectively evaluate the social competence of pupils, just as the elementary-classroom teacher does. The physical educator's evaluation of the status and progress of primary-grade pupils must be subjective. Anecdotal reports may be made to parents.

It is generally agreed that the elementary-classroom teacher should supplement the teaching of physical education by the physical educator. Since the elementary-classroom teacher should be teaching some of the physical education to her pupils, she should be involved in evaluating her pupil's status and progress in physical education. The cooperative effort of both the physical educator and the classroom teacher will result in a sound and comprehensive evaluation of the pupils.

THIRD SITUATION:
REPORTING TEST SCORES TO PARENTS

The physical education staff at Harper High School administers the AAHPER Fitness Test to all pupils. The administration has asked the staff how the findings can best be interpreted to the parents and who should communicate the information.

QUESTIONS

What means of communication does the school have with parents? Can physical-fitness test results best be communicated orally, in writing, or both? Who should have the responsibility for interpreting physical-fitness test results to the parents?

ANALYSIS

There are several means of communication that school personnel have with parents, including conferences, P.T.A. meetings, report cards, demonstrations, progress reports, and television and radio programs. One of the most effective ways of interpreting any phase of physical education is by demonstration.

Probably, both oral and written communication of test results should be used. An excellent technique for informing parents of their pupil's progress in physical fitness is to send home a report explaining the test and the results of their child's performance. Both the administration and the physical education staff have the responsibility for communicating with the parents about all phases of the physical education program. However, because of the technical nature of the interpretation of physical fitness test scores, this responsibility should belong to the physical education staff, which has the requisite professional background.

FOURTH SITUATION: A MARKING PLAN

The physical education teachers at Hudson High School have been asked to submit a plan to the high-school principal for marking pupils in physical education. Mr. Raush, the directory of physical education, has asked his staff to come to its monthly meeting next Tuesday with some suggestions.

QUESTIONS

What factors should be considered by the staff in developing a marking system for physical education? Should a marking system be numerical, letter, or Satisfactory–Unsatisfactory? Should the physical education mark be included in figuring averages for the honor roll?

ANALYSIS

The marking system should be based upon the objectives of physical education and should include the following: physical fitness, skills, knowledge, and social competence. These aspects of performance may be measured subjectively as well as objectively. The staff must determine what weight to give each of these objectives in determining a mark in physical education, by deciding their relative value.

A marking system for physical education in a school should be consistent with the marking system in other subjects. If English, social studies, and science are marked numerically, then physical education should be marked numerically.

Since physical education is part of the total curriculum and can be measured like other subjects, it should be included with other subjects in figuring the average for the honor roll. Pupils must be totally educated, in both mind and body, and it is imperative to avoid dichotomizing the individual.

FIFTH SITUATION:
FAILING IN PHYSICAL EDUCATION

Sally Smith, a senior in Jonesville High School, has received a failing mark in physical education. Her parents are quite concerned because it is the only course she is failing and it is keeping her off the honor roll. They have contacted Mr. Kinsey, the high school principal, who invited them to the school to talk to Miss Burns, the physical education teacher.

QUESTIONS

What should constitute a passing mark in physical education? Has the school informed the parents as to what is passing or failing in physical education? Had Sally's parents been informed previous to this marking period as to her status in physical education?

ANALYSIS

Marks in physical education should be based upon the objectives of the program. Therefore, tests and other evaluative techniques should be used to measure physical fitness, skills, knowledges, and social competence. All of these evaluative techniques should take into consideration individual differences among pupils. A pupil who attends class, participates in the activities, cooperates, and works to his capacity should be able to attain the minimum standard for passing physical education.

The school should inform the parents about the physical education program including policies pursuant to such topics as passing and failing. This can be done in a number of different ways, including parent conferences, letters, and handbooks. Another source of information that would assist parents, as well as other teachers, board of education members, and administrators in the understanding of physical education is a local course of study.

There should be a periodic report of pupil status and progress sent to the parents so that they are informed. Prior to receiving a failing grade in physical education, there should have been conferences between the pupil and Miss Burns and also between Sally's parents and Miss Burns.

SIXTH SITUATION: PHYSICAL-FITNESS TESTS

At a physical education staff meeting there is a discussion of physical-fitness testing. One of the teachers says that a real good test of physical fitness is the Rogers Physical Fitness Index and that it should be administered throughout the school district for both boys and girls. Another teacher disagrees and states that a better test for measuring the physical fitness of boys and girls is Larson's Dynamic Strength Test. The final decision must be made by Mr. Phelan, the director of physical education. What test should he select?

QUESTIONS

For what grade level are these tests recommended? Are they recommended for both boys and girls? Do they require expensive equipment? Can they be administered in a minimum amount of time? What components of physical fitness do they measure?

ANALYSIS

The Rogers Physical Fitness Index is recommended for boys and girls, ages 8 to 18. The Larson Dynamic Strength Test is recommended for high school boys only. On this basis, the better test for Mr. Phelan would be the Rogers Physical Fitness Index. With it, his school district could measure the performance of all pupils in grades 4 to 12 with the same test.

The Rogers Physical Fitness Index takes a considerable amount of expensive equipment, however, and it takes a great deal of time to administer and score, while the Larson Dynamic Strength Test uses only the high horizontal bar and the parallel bars, which most high schools should have. This test is much shorter than the Physical Fitness Index and therefore can be given in much less time.

Both tests chiefly measure strength, and the newer concept of physical fitness is broader. Other factors, such as agility, speed, and endurance, should be considered components of physical fitness. Mr. Phelan should therefore look for a more comprehensive test than either of the two suggested at the meeting.

DISCUSSION NOTES

**PERSONAL PRACTICE-TEACHING EXPERIENCE
RELATED TO TOPIC**

SELECTED REFERENCES

BARROW, HAROLD M., and ROSEMARY McGEE, *A Practical Approach to Measurement in Physical Education.* Philadelphia: Lea & Febiger, 1964.

BOVARD, J. F., F. W. COZENS, and E. P. HAGMAN, *Tests and Measurements in Physical Education* (3rd ed.). Philadelphia: W. B. Saunders Company, 1949.

CLARKE, H. HARRISON, *Application of Measurement to Health and Physical Education.* Englewood Cliffs, N.J.: Prentice-Hall, Inc., 1967.

MATTHEWS, DONALD K., *Measurement in Physical Education.* Philadelphia: W. B. Saunders Company, 1963.

MEYERS, CARLTON R., and T. E. BLESH, *Measurement in Physical Education.* New York: The Ronald Press Company, 1962.

SCOTT, M. GLADYS, and ESTHER FRENCH, *Measurement and Evaluation in Physical Education.* Dubuque: Wm. C. Brown Co., 1959.

WILGOOSE, C. E., *Evaluation in Health and Physical Education.* New York: McGraw-Hill Book Company, 1961.

LET ME INTRODUCE OUR NEW PHYSICAL EDUCATION TEACHER
PTA MEETING
WE NEVER HAD A CROWD THIS LARGE BEFORE

Public Relations
CHAPTER 11

There is general agreement among authors that today's concept of public relations grew out of the word "publicity." In order to gain public understanding and support from the community, however, it is necessary to do more than publicize the program of physical education. It is necessary to make use of the many desirable methods of leading public opinion toward intelligent group action and support of the physical education program. This makes it necessary to create a two-way avenue for communication, so that information and understanding can travel between the personnel in the schools and the citizens of the community.

THE FUNCTIONS OF PUBLIC RELATIONS

Some of the more important functions of public relations, as they relate to the physical education program, are:

☐ To keep the community properly informed about all parts of the physical education program.

☐ To develop an awareness of the need for a good physical education program in the total educational curriculum.

☐ To gain support for adequate facilities, sufficient teaching time, and qualified personnel.

☐ To promote the concept of the united action of teachers and parents for a better physical education program.
☐ To evaluate the physical education program as to whether it is meeting the needs of pupils in the community.
☐ To avoid any misunderstandings about the aims and objectives of the physical education program.

PRINCIPLES OF PUBLIC RELATIONS

A good public relations program for physical education must be based on sound principles:

☐ Accuracy.
☐ Awareness of the fact that there are many different publics, with varying interests and problems.
☐ A good physical education program.
☐ Continuity.
☐ Two-way communication of information between the school and the community.
☐ A knowledge of what the community thinks about the physical education program.
☐ Involvement of all school personnel.

COMMUNICATION WITH VARIOUS PUBLICS

Physical education is often questioned as an academic subject, and so is its place in the total educational program. Although everyone outside of the field claims to know something about it, the interesting fact is that people know very little about physical education.

Many misconceptions and half-truths handicap the program of physical education. There are several publics that need to know the facts. The best way to get the facts to them is for physical educators to communicate what is being done and what they hope to do. There are many ways that a physical educator can promote his program with the various publics. Some of these are:

☐ Teach your pupils what physical education is and how it can help them. Proper communication with pupils will teach them what it means to be physically educated, and they will learn to appreciate and respect skilled movements and a strong, healthy body.

☐ Keep the parents informed about what you are doing with their children in the physical education program. The average parent is as concerned with the class-instruction activities as he is with the extra-class activities.

☐ Socialize with other faculty members outside of physical education. Go to lunch with them, serve on committees, and make it a point to attend all faculty meetings. Try to learn what is happening in other subjects and the problems that are being encountered. The physical educator should be sympathetic and understanding of others' problems if he is to expect the same treatment from them.

☐ Keep all administrators informed about the program of physical education. One of the best ways is for the physical education staff to develop a local course of study which is submitted to the administration and board of education.

☐ Inform the board of education about the physical education program, objectives, and problems. This can be done by presenting an annual report to the board of education and also by submitting copies of a local course of study.

PUBLIC-RELATIONS MEDIA

There are numerous media of communications which can be used in a public-relations program. Two factors should determine what media should be used in a particular situation: (1) certain media have more significance than others in a particular community; and (2) certain media are more readily available than others. The physical education staff should make a survey of its situation to determine which media can be used and which will do the most effective job. However, it should never be forgotten that the best way of building good public relations is still through the program and the leadership.

NEWSPAPERS

The newspaper is one of the most common and useful media for disseminating information. It reaches many people and can be of great assistance in interpreting the physical education program to the community. When preparing news stories:

☐ State only the facts.
☐ Tell the story briefly.
☐ Make the report coherent and accurate.
☐ Punctuate and paragraph correctly.
☐ Avoid abbreviations, slang, wordiness, and involved sentences.

- ☐ Type the copy with double spacing.
- ☐ Make sure that your story is in on time.

PHOTOGRAPHS AND GRAPHICS

Both pictures and graphic illustrations are very effective. Photographs should show action and include people: Action pictures are more appealing than static ones and pictures with people in them are more effective than pictures that do not have people. Usually, a few people are better than many persons.—e.g., physical-fitness scores and number of participants in the intramural and interscholastic activities—can be made more interesting and appealing if they are presented in graphs, charts, and profiles.

PUBLIC SPEECHES

Making speeches to the public can be a very effective medium for public relations. A good speech will often do much to inform the public about the physical education program. To develop an effective speech:

- ☐ Know the purpose of the speech.
- ☐ Know what public will be listening.
- ☐ Prepare a general outline of the speech.
- ☐ Research and collect information for the speech.
- ☐ Prepare a more detailed outline of the speech.
- ☐ Practice the speech.

FILMS

Films are a very effective way of presenting a story in a short period of time. The 8 and 16-millimeter film can be used by the physical education staff to show the public exactly what is being done in the physical education program. Movies can be taken of activities during physical education classes for showing at PTA meetings. Films are also a good instructional aid in working with pupils.

RADIO AND TELEVISION

Because of their universal appeal, radio and television are very effective means of communication. These media offer the best opportunity to reach the greatest number of people at one time. Some radio and television stations will make free time available as a public service. In some communities there are educational radio and television stations. Some schools are fortunate enough to have stations of their own.

DISPLAYS

Posters, exhibits, and brochures can be used to advertise, promote, announce, recognize, and dramatize the program. Almost every school has bulletin boards in the physical education areas. Very effective use can be made of these bulletin boards by:

- ☐ Making the display attractive, bright, colorful, and eye-catching.
- ☐ Using clippings and pictures.
- ☐ Printing in large letters.
- ☐ Posting up-to-date information about activities, times, places, persons to see.

LIVE DEMONSTRATIONS

Demonstrations at which all pupils perform are an entertaining and informative medium for public relations. For an effective presentation:

- ☐ Use student leaders for demonstration purposes, to demonstrate your teaching of leadership.
- ☐ Make the demonstration dynamic, interesting, and informative.
- ☐ Explain the objectives of the program as the pupils perform.
- ☐ Make sure that all safety precautions have been followed.
- ☐ Keep the program short enough so that it doesn't drag.

public relations: situations and analysis

FIRST SITUATION: STAR PERFORMERS

Mr. Doherty, the principal of the Henry C. Calhoun Elementary School, wants the parents to have a better understanding of the various special educational programs in his school. He is asking Miss Carr, the physical education teacher, to have a few highly skilled pupils perform for the P.T.A. Miss Carr questions whether this approach will promote the best public relations.

QUESTIONS

Is the use of a few skilled performers the best way of informing the public about the program of physical education? What other ways can pupils be used to inform the public about physical education?

ANALYSIS

The use of a few skilled performers is one way of communicating the physical education program to the public. The limitation of this method, well exemplified by interscholastic athletics, is that you reach a limited number of parents and are usually presenting only a limited portion of the program. When only a few skilled performers and a limited number of activities are presented, the public is misinformed about the total physical education program.

There are several other ways that pupils may be used to inform the public about physical education. Probably the best advertisement for the school is the child who goes home each day happy, motivated, and well-informed. This can only be accomplished with a curriculum that meets his interests and needs, and challenges his capacities—and a well-taught, broad physical education program including many activities is an essential part of such a curriculum.

Live demonstrations at P.T.A. meetings, open house, and other school-community functions are an excellent means of using the pupils to communicate with the public. These demonstrations should include all pupils in the everyday classes, however, and not just the highly skilled.

The intramural program is a valuable part of the extra-class program and it can also be used effectively to better inform the public. A few of the intramural contests for boys and girls should be scheduled in the evening, so parents can attend.

SECOND SITUATION:
BULLETIN BOARDS

Mr. Beam, the director of physical education, is concerned because the physical education teachers in his two senior-high schools and six junior-high schools are not using the physical education bulletin boards as a means of promoting the program of physical education.

QUESTIONS

What use can be made of the bulletin boards as a means of public relations? What factors should be considered?

ANALYSIS

Since bulletin boards are generally strategically located near the gymnasium or the dressing and showering facilities, they can be very effectively used for public relations. Among the many uses of a bulletin board are: advertising, promotions, announcements, recognition, and dramatization. Probably the best use of bulletin boards however, is to display educational materials. Such information as the position of players, the location of facilities, supplies, and equipment, and the meaning of terminology can be presented. Unfortunately, too few bulletin boards display such materials.

Certain factors make for an effective bulletin board. Materials should be attractive, bright, colorful, and eye-catching. The printing or writing should be in large-enough letters to be readable at short distances. The bulletin board should be kept up-to-date by changing the information about different schedules, places, persons, and activities each season.

THIRD SITUATION: A FOOTBALL FILM

Mr. Gainey, the superintendent of schools, has asked Mr. Sager, the director of physical education, to show the film of last Saturday's football game to the Rotary Club on Thursday evening. He has indicated to Mr. Sager that this would be an excellent means for explaining the physical education program to the public.

QUESTIONS

Is the showing of a film a desirable means of public relations? Why is it desirable to use public-relations media with community service organizations? Is the showing of a high-school football film the most desirable way of interpreting the physical education program to the public?

ANALYSIS

Since a great many people enjoy watching films, it is one of the better ways of keeping the public well informed. Films are not only entertaining but also are an effective vehicle for information and education. Films can build up interest, capture attention, and stimulate thinking in ways not possible with printed materials.

It is desirable to use public-relations media with community-service organizations because the members of such clubs are interested in the welfare of their children and in the schools. Since many of these organizations ask school personnel to present programs at their meetings, they provide ready-made situations where publicity can be truly effective. Generally speaking, members of service clubs are the leaders and influential people in the community. Because of their position and interest, they can do much to further a school's relation with the general public.

A high-school football film is one way to show part of the physical education program, but showing only one activity is not the best way to interpret the physical education program to the public. A better procedure would be to show a film of boys and girls in all grades participating in many different activities in their everyday physical education classes. Such a film would show class activities, intramurals, and interscholastics.

FOURTH SITUATION:
A NEWSPAPER STORY

Mr. Ravena, the new director of physical education in the Batavia City School District, has noticed that there are several errors in an article about the physical education program in the city newspaper.

QUESTIONS

What steps should be taken by the director of physical education to insure that a newspaper story is accurate? What sources of information should reporters use in writing articles about physical education?

ANALYSIS

Because the newspaper is one of the most common and useful media for informing the public, great care should be taken to insure accuracy. The director of physical education should keep the story brief and state only the facts. After it has been written it should be checked to see that it is coherent, properly punctuated, and paragraphed correctly. Abbreviations, slang, wordiness, and involved sentences should be avoided. The final copy should be typewritten, with double spacing, and submitted on time.

There are various sources of information available to reporters who may write articles about physical education. Physical education teachers can be encouraged to write about the physical education activities in their schools. The coaches of interscholastic athletics can give first-hand information about their teams. All stories should clear through the school principal, the director of physical education, and the superintendent before release.

FIFTH SITUATION: SHOWERS

Miss Welker, the physical education teacher at Cooperstown High School, would like to have all girls shower at the end of the physical education classes now that adequate facilities are available in the new high school. After the first week of classes, Miss Welker has noticed that many girls are not taking showers.

QUESTIONS

What are the first steps that Miss Welker should take in order to properly implement the showering phase of the program? What action should she take with the pupils who are not showering? Besides the pupils, what other people should be informed about showering as an integral part of the program?

ANALYSIS

In order to properly implement the showering phase of the program, Miss Welker should first discuss the value of this program with the pupils. She should check to see if facilities exist in the elementary grades and junior-high school grades, and whether the girls are using them.

Miss Welker should find out why the girls are not taking showers. It may be that they feel too rushed. The teacher should then allocate more time, if she feels that this is a reasonable complaint. If it is a question of modesty, individual stall showers would help. If they are not available and not many girls are affected, these girls might be excused early so that they could shower before the rest of the class.

Parents should be informed that showering is an integral part of the program, because many times the problem is not with the child but with the parents. It is easier to carry out any program if the teacher has the cooperation of both the parent and the child.

SIXTH SITUATION:
A P.T.A. TALK

Mrs. Bigsbee, the physical education teacher in Fly Creek Elementary School, has been asked by her principal, Mr. Herman, to give a speech at the next P.T.A. meeting on the values of a good physical education program.

QUESTIONS

What can Mrs. Bigsbee do to help develop an effective speech? What are some of the fundamentals of a good speech?

ANALYSIS

There are several things Mrs. Bigsbee can do to help develop an effective speech. First, she must decide the purpose of her speech and find out who will be her audience. Then she should prepare a general outline of her speech. Once this is done, she should read the literature and start to glean information for the speech. She could then develop a more detailed outline of her speech. Last, she should practice the speech several times.

There are several fundamentals of a good speech. The speaker should know his subject thoroughly. He should exhibit great interest in and enthusiasm for his topic. His main effort should be to put ideas and facts across to the audience, rather than to put himself across. The speech should be well prepared, direct, not too lengthy, and clear.

SELECTED REFERENCES

American Association for Health, Physical Education and Recreation, *Putting the PR into HPER*. Washington, D.C.: National Education Association, 1953.

American Association of School Administrators, *Public Relations for America's Schools*. Washington, D.C.: National Education Association, 1950.

BERNAYS, EDWARD L., *Public Relations.* Norman: University of Oklahoma Press, 1952.

DOOB, LEONARD W., *Public Opinion and Propaganda.* New York: Holt, Rinehart and Winston, Inc., 1948.

GUNNING, ROBERT, *The Technique of Clear Writing.* New York: McGraw-Hill Book Company, 1952.

PLACKARD, DWIGHT HILLIS, and CLIFTON BLACKMAN, *Blueprint for Public Relations.* New York: McGraw-Hill Book Company, 1947.

The Evaluation of Student Teaching

CHAPTER 12

A COOPERATIVE EFFORT

In order for the evaluation of student teaching to be effective, it must include appraisals by the supervising teacher, college supervisor, and student teacher. Additional valuable information may be obtained from pupils, physical education department chairmen, and principals.

The student teacher should learn to think critically about his own accomplishments. When he does, there is developed a sound foundation upon which continuous growth can be built. The supervising teacher and the college supervisor should assist the student teacher to analyze himself objectively and to develop a sincere desire to improve the quality of his teaching. When evaluation is a cooperative effort, it should motivate the student teacher to develop his own potentialities.

There should be an evaluation of errors, primarily for the growth that comes with avoiding and overcoming them. It must be remembered that the main purpose of student teaching is to further growth of the student, not to judge him as if he were a master teacher.

PURPOSES OF EVALUATION

The purposes of evaluation of student teaching in physical education are:

- ☐ To provide a foundation for a cooperative relationship for the continuous growth and development of the student teacher.

- ☐ To provide motivation so that the student teacher has a desire for self-appraisal and self-evaluation.
- ☐ To determine the strengths, weaknesses, and readiness of the student teacher so he may be better prepared for his teaching assignments.
- ☐ To determine the status and progress of the student teacher.
- ☐ To provide a measure of prediction of future success as a teacher.

PRINCIPLES OF EVALUATION

Several principles are basic to the sound evaluation of student teaching:

- ☐ The primary purpose of evaluation is to make desirable changes.
- ☐ Evaluation must be based upon a set of objectives mutually accepted by the supervising teacher, college supervisor, and student teacher.
- ☐ Evaluation must be a cooperative effort and lead to self-evaluation.
- ☐ Evaluation is an essential part of the learning process and must be continuous.
- ☐ A variety of methods, including measures of quality and quantity, must be used for collecting the evidence upon which the evaluation is based.
- ☐ Evaluation must clearly indicate both the effort and achievement of the student teacher.
- ☐ Evaluation is not a separate aspect, but an integral part of the total student-teaching experience.
- ☐ Evaluation must be based upon sound principles of learning.

TECHNIQUES OF EVALUATION

One of the most important techniques in the evaluation of student teaching is the daily conference between the student teacher and the supervising teacher. Additional evaluation is made in conferences between the college supervisor and the student teacher.

It is during these conferences that the student teacher should receive guidance from the professional staff who give leadership and direction to his growth as a student teacher. Many times, it is the conference that allows the student teacher to gain greater insight into the relationship between theory and practice. These conferences should also serve as a basis for self-appraisal and self-evaluation.

In addition to the conference, there are other valuable techniques which should be used to evaluate the student-teaching experience. One of the greatest weaknesses in the evaluation of the student-teaching experience is the use of a single device for evaluation. Some techniques that are presently used for a comprehensive evaluation are: autobiographies, teaching records, rating scales, case studies, checklists, activity charts, weekly reports, teaching plans, questionnaires, group discussions, and observations. There is great similarity in the forms used in various colleges and universities because the information used in their construction is based upon the four general areas of: (1) personal qualities; (2) professional qualities; (3) human relations; and (4) communication skills.

As we have already indicated, evaluation, to be truly effective, must be a cooperative effort of all concerned, including the student teacher, supervising teacher, college supervisor, and pupils. Following are illustrations of some typical evaluative forms used by these different individuals.

THE STUDENT TEACHER

In order to assist a student teacher in his self-evaluation, many colleges and universities use a self-rating scale. The two reproduced here are used at Arnold College of the University of Bridgeport, and Arizona State University at Tempe, respectively.

ARNOLD COLLEGE DIVISION, UNIVERSITY OF BRIDGEPORT

*SELF-RATING SCALE FOR STUDENT TEACHERS.**

It is important that continuous improvement be made by a student in his role as a teacher. Pupils will be "rating" you throughout each day, even though their appraisals may be somewhat disorganized. The following scale should help guide self-appraisal and assist you in terms of professional growth.

Interpret the qualities mentioned in terms of:
Always; Usually; Occasionally; or *Rarely* (if ever).

*Reprinted with permission from the Arnold College Division of the University of Bridgeport; Bridgeport, Connecticut.

RELATIONSHIPS WITH CLASS. Are you:
_____ Cross, grouchy, sarcastic, mean
_____ Unreasonable, intolerant
_____ Pleasant, good natured, inclined not to lose temper often
_____ Kindly, seldom angry
_____ Cheerful, happy, possessed with a sense of humor

PRESENTATIONS. Are your explanations:
_____ Always clear, thorough, and easy to understand by all
_____ So well presented that all but a few grasp the meaning
_____ Understood by at least a majority of the class
_____ Understood by only a few of the best pupils
_____ So confusing that no one understands

FAIRNESS. Are you:
_____ Treating everybody with fairness
_____ Fair to all except the worst troublemakers
_____ Fair to the majority of the pupils
_____ Rather unfair to all except those who "play up" to you
_____ Too partial, unfair, tending to have "pets"

CLASSROOM MANAGEMENT. Have you found that:
_____ You have no control over pupils; class is very disorderly
_____ Most of the class is disorderly
_____ Most of the class is orderly and cooperative
_____ All but a few troublemakers are orderly and cooperative
_____ You have excellent control over pupils; class is well behaved and cooperative

PROMOTION OF INTEREST. Have you found that:
_____ You make the subject extremely tiresome and boring
_____ Nearly all of the pupils lack interest
_____ Most of the pupils are interested
_____ All but a few of the pupils find the subject interesting
_____ You make the subject very interesting and worthwhile to all pupils

KNOWLEDGE OF THE SUBJECT. Have you found that you:
_____ Know the subject thoroughly; seldom make a mistake
_____ Know the subject rather well; mistakes do not interfere with effectiveness
_____ Are generally well-informed concerning the subject
_____ Don't know the subject well enough; are sometimes confused
_____ Do not know the subject; make mistakes frequently

ARIZONA STATE UNIVERSITY AT TEMPE

*SELF-EVALUATION DEVICE FOR STUDENT TEACHERS**

Mark each item with "O" for outstanding, "S" for satisfactory, "N" for needs improvement. If the item has not been encountered, leave blank.

	1st Half	2nd Half
A. UNDERSTANDS SELF		
1. Sees teaching as a professional endeavor		
2. Motivated by desire to build self-satisfaction through service to others		
3. Well enough adjusted so that does not need to make pupils uncomfortable to be happy		
4. Personal appearance		
Well groomed		
Dresses properly		
5. Health		
6. Personal characteristics		
Posture		
Poise		
No disturbing mannerisms		
Enthusiasm		
Sincerity		
Pleasing voice		
Sense of humor		
Sensitivity to feelings of others		
Establishes satisfactory relations		
7. Initiative		
Sees possibilities for helping and goes ahead without being asked		
Meets emergencies calmly		
8. Progresses in ability to evaluate self as a teacher		
9. Maintains a business-like class atmosphere		
10. Familiar with trends in education		

*Reprinted with permission from the Department of Health, Physical Education and Recreation, Arizona State University, Tempe, Arizona.

11. Has a working acquaintance with professional literature ____
12. Has an awareness of national and world problems ____

B. UNDERSTANDS PUPILS
   1. Interested in pupils and recognizes individual differences ____
   2. Knows how to study pupils as individuals and groups ____
   3. Knows how to gather data on pupils ____
   4. Knows how to utilize data ____
   5. Knows how to communicate with pupils ____
   6. Knows basic information about normal development of age group of pupils ____

C. UNDERSTANDS THE COMMUNITY
   1. Studies community problems and needs ____
   2. Works on a basis of cooperation and mutual understanding with community groups and organizations ____
   3. Takes part in school programs to improve the community ____
   4. Uses the community in improving the curriculum ____
   5. Knows the basic ideals and values of democratic living ____
   6. Visits homes of pupils ____
   7. Considers patterns and customs of individuals and groups in community ____

D. UNDERSTANDS THE SCHOOL
   1. Studies the roles and responsibilities of co-workers in the school
      Teachers ____
      Principal ____
      Nurse ____
      Counselors ____
      Secretary ____
      Bus Driver ____
      Custodian ____
      Cafeteria helper ____
      Attendance Officer ____
   2. Attends faculty meetings and contributes to them ____
   3. Attends and contributes to committee meetings ____
   4. Attends and contributes to P.T.A. Meetings ____
   5. Upholds school customs and policies ____
   6. Is accurate and prompt in submitting materials ____
   7. Is friendly, respectful and cooperative with other teachers ____
   8. Assumes responsibility for extra-duty and housekeeping routines ____
   9. Is aware of the effect of scheduling upon curriculums ____

10. Displays initiative which is the foundation of democratic administration _____

E. IDENTIFYING, DEFINING AND USING OBJECTIVES
   1. Understands cooperative purposing, planning, performing, and appraising _____
   2. Knows the function of objectives in curriculum and instruction _____
   3. Knows the commonly accepted objectives of elementary and secondary schools _____
   4. Can generalize on the basis of needs and plan the balanced growth of the group _____
   5. Can translate needs into desired behaviors for curriculum and instruction objectives _____
   6. Uses knowledges and capabilities in identifying and defining objectives _____

F. SELECTING LEARNING
   1. Understands what type of experiences are consistent with learning principles, the needs of the pupils and a democratic society _____
   2. Realizes the degree to which pre-planning is necessary and useful _____
   3. Guides cooperative planning with children in setting up goals and selecting experiences _____
   4. Guides children in selecting and organizing needed information _____
   5. Plans and helps to provide stimulating and pleasant learning environment _____

G. GUIDING AND DEVELOPING THE LEARNING ACTIVITIES
   1. Plans resource units _____
   2. Helps pupils identify goals _____
   3. Uses classroom experiences as a basis for the guidance of pupils _____
   4. Makes the classroom a center of varied learning activities. Uses audio materials (radio, phonograph, tape) _____
      Uses visual materials _____
      Uses school library _____
      Uses supplementary reading materials _____
      Uses people who are informed _____
      Organizes committees for work on problems _____
      Organizes excursions _____
      Provides for special reports to class _____
      Provides for summarizing or culminating activities _____

182 STUDENT TEACHING: HOW, WHEN?

  5. Makes clear and definite assignments _____
  6. Is flexible to adjusting plans to changing attitudes _____
  7. Guides students in managing time _____

 H. EVALUATING THE RESULTS OF LEARNING
  1. Evaluates and appraises the extent to which learners and the school have achieved purposes _____
  2. Evaluates in terms of the learner's pattern and rates of growth _____
  3. Provides opportunity for self-evaluation by the learners _____
  4. Evaluates through day to day observation of behavior _____
  5. Evaluates with a view toward improving means and ends _____
  6. Recognizes that ultimate evaluation waits upon behavior in life _____
  7. Recognizes the subjective as well as the objective nature of evaluation _____
  8. Progresses in ability to evaluate self as a teacher _____

SUPERVISING TEACHER

Many colleges and universities use various techniques to assist supervising teachers in evaluating themselves and their student teachers. Some of the more valuable instruments used are checklists for supervising teachers and checklists for student teachers. The following are used at University of Minnesota and Iowa State University at Ames, respectively.

IOWA STATE UNIVERSITY, TEACHER EDUCATION

FINAL EVALUATION OF STUDENT TEACHING*

Instructions. Please place a check mark in the space adjacent to the alternative that best describes your student teacher in relation to others with

*Reprinted with permission from the College of Education, Iowa State University, Ames, Iowa.

comparable experience. Should you find it impossible to choose a particular description, provision is made for checking half-way between two items.

PERSONAL QUALIFICATIONS

A. *Appearance*
 _____ 1. Always well groomed; appropriately dressed; shows good taste
 _____ 2. Generally acceptable in dress and appearance; could be improved occasionally
 _____ 3. Poor taste in dress and grooming, careless; occasionally sloppy
 _____ 4. No comment; no opportunity to judge

B. *Health and Vitality*
 _____ 1. Excellent health; seldom absent due to illness; unlimited energy
 _____ 2. Good health; ample energy for teaching demands; adequate vitality
 _____ 3. Chronically ill; excessive absences; physical handicaps impede effectiveness
 _____ 4. No comment; no opportunity to judge

C. *Voice and Communication*
 _____ 1. Pleasing voice; excellent vocabulary; proper inflection, volume, etc.
 _____ 2. Usually speaks well; easily understood; adequate volume, tone, etc.
 _____ 3. Inaudible; lacks force; hard to understand; excessive errors in English
 _____ 4. No comment; no opportunity to judge

D. *Emotional Stability*
 _____ 1. Poised; good sense of humor; handles the unexpected with ease
 _____ 2. Usually well-controlled; has occasional moods, but none extreme
 _____ 3. Excessive moodiness; easily irritated; apathetic; avoids reality
 _____ 4. No comment; no opportunity to judge

E. *Responsibility and Dependability*
_____ 1. Always reliable and on time; resourceful; frequently seeks more responsibility

_____ 2. Usually does the expected; generally dependable; follows directions well

_____ 3. Negligent in carrying out duties; very unpredictable; does only enough to get by

_____ 4. No comment; no opportunity to judge

F. *Interpersonal Relationships*
_____ 1. Very friendly; harmonious and honest; well-liked by faculty and students

_____ 2. Moderately effective in social situations; generally relates well; accepted

_____ 3. Aloof; cold and cynical; too familiar or too distant; irritates others

_____ 4. No comment; no opportunity to judge

PROFESSIONAL QUALIFICATIONS

A. *Knowledge of Subject Matter*
_____ 1. Extremely well prepared; thorough mastery of material; knowledgeable

_____ 2. Appears sufficiently competent; recognizes deficiencies; seeks to fill voids

_____ 3. Inadequately prepared in area; knowledge is limited; vague and inaccurate

_____ 4. No comment; no opportunity to judge

B. *Desire to Teach*
_____ 1. Very enthusiastic; anxious to enter profession; serious in purpose

_____ 2. Moderately interested; sometimes questions teaching as career; ambivalent

_____ 3. Seriously questions purpose; views teaching as insurance; bored and disinterested

_____ 4. No comment; no opportunity to judge

C. *Attitude toward Constructive Criticism*
   _____ 1. Always welcomes suggestions; solicits help; profits from assistance

   _____ 2. Accepts suggestions; generally makes effort to improve; seldom balks

   _____ 3. Resists assistance; confused; tends to overlook suggestions

   _____ 4. No comment; no opportunity to judge

D. *Interest in Community Relations*
   _____ 1. Considerable involvement; shows interest and enthusiasm for civic affairs

   _____ 2. Maintains casual interest; occasionally participates in community affairs

   _____ 3. No apparent contact with community; disinterested; avoids local involvement

   _____ 4. No comment; no opportunity to judge

CLASSROOM COMPETENCIES AND TECHNIQUES

A. *Planning*
   _____ 1. Fully developed and consistent; exhibits originality; employs variety

   _____ 2. Generally adequate; usually well organized; needs only occasional direction

   _____ 3. Very sketchy; lacks organization and continuity; inadequate goals

   _____ 4. No comment; no opportunity to judge

B. *Concepts and Generalizations*
   _____ 1. Full development of concepts; relationships clear; generalizations understood

   _____ 2. Concepts generally developed; relationships usually clear and understood

   _____ 3. Concepts seldom fully developed; relationships hazy; understanding doubtful

   _____ 4. No comment; no opportunity to judge

C. *Ability to Analyze Learning Problems*
   _____ 1. Anticipates problems; selects materials wisely; provides for individual needs

   _____ 2. Aware of problems; relies on regular teacher; employs suggested materials

   _____ 3. Fails to recognize problems; ignores ability differences; book oriented

   _____ 4. No comment; no opportunity to judge

D. *Classroom Management*
   _____ 1. Seldom has discipline problems; anticipates difficulties; fair and firm

   _____ 2. Satisfactorily attends to routine; appropriate order and respect, usually consistent

   _____ 3. Poor classroom control; frequent problems; vacillates, too strict or too free

   _____ 4. No comment; no opportunity to judge

E. *Measurement and Evaluation*
   _____ 1. Always based on worthwhile purposes; encourages self-evaluation; tests are comprehensive, yet reasonable

   _____ 2. Evaluative devices generally satisfactory; occasionally uses tests results for re-teaching in later lessons

   _____ 3. Poorly designed tests; evaluation seldom appropriate to objectives; results recorded and ignored

   _____ 4. No comment; no opportunity to judge

PROFESSIONAL JUDGMENT OF STUDENT TEACHER'S POTENTIALITY

   _____ 1. Student teacher has done an exceptionally good job; with a little more opportunity for professional growth that will come from having a job of his own, he is almost certain to become an outstanding teacher.

   _____ 2. Student teacher has done a very good job. I am convinced that he will be an asset to whatever school system may hire him and may even become an outstanding teacher in time.

   _____

_____ 3. Student teacher has done a reasonably good job and I feel that he is now competent to handle a classroom of his own satisfactorily.

_____ 4. Student teacher is making progress and shows promise; for his own good, however, it would probably be best if in his first position he could continue to receive close supervision and support for a while longer.

_____ 5. Student teacher falls short of being ready to take on a regular teaching position; he needs further improvement before I could honestly predict for him success in the teaching profession.

**UNIVERSITY OF MINNESOTA
SCHOOL OF PHYSICAL EDUCATION AND RECREATION
DEPARTMENT OF PHYSICAL EDUCATION FOR MEN**

*STUDENT TEACHING SUMMARY**

NAME _____

To the Supervising Teacher: Please check each question to the best of your ability; according to the student's performance as a student teacher this quarter.

How does his personal appearance impress you?	Makes poor impression	Average impression	Excellent appearance, always well groomed
How does he interact with people?	Antagonizes and irritates others	Gets along well	Especially harmonious relations with others
Is he well poised?	Too easily moved to anger	Usually well controlled	Relaxed and confident

*Reprinted with permission of James E. Torpey, Department of Physical Education for Men, University of Minnesota.

Is his manner of speech acceptable?	Makes frequent errors in speech; expression poor		Communicates reasonably well; English usually good	Excellent English; conveys ideas effectively
How does he communicate with the children?	Poor selection of words, terms, descriptions		Simple, concise and easy to understand	Especially appropriate for the age level
What is his attitude toward children?	Dominates, decides everything		Encourages participation whenever possible	Encourages pupil initiative; guidance approach evident
What is the atmosphere of his teaching situations?	Children seldom concentrate and work		Children show interest	Children are interested, motivated, and inspired
How does he control unexpected situations?	Baffled; poor decisions, loses control		Meets emergencies fairly well	Anticipates emergencies, prevents problems
Are his lessons well-planned?	Seldom shows evidence of planning		Lessons well planned	Careful, cooperatively formulated plans
Does he meet his lesson objectives?	Doesn't try to evaluate		Sometimes meets objectives	Always meets objectives
How does he organize his classes?	Rigid planning		Makes allowances for flexibility	Is keenly aware of necessary changes and makes them
Is he skillful in class management?	Confused about where to begin and what to do		Established routine fairly well	Always has things under control
Does he plan so that all children are active most of the time?	Too much waiting in lines and listening to directions		Most lessons planned so all children are engaged in activities	All children are always engaged in activities

Does he show evidence of individualizing instructions?	All children are treated alike most of the time		Often makes allowance		Always makes provisions for individual differences
What use does he make of materials of instruction?	Uses what is available		Supplements available materials to some extent		Uses a wide variety of source material
How does he provide for supplies and equipment?	Neglects equipment and supplies		Keeps things in order		Excellent care of equipment and supplies
Does he show resourcefulness, initiative and ambition?	Requires prodding; shirks responsibility		Works conscientiously but requires constant help		Finds things to do without supervision
How does he react to suggestions and criticism?	Is offended		Accepts them and performs accordingly		Cooperates cheerfully and seeks help when needed
Does he possess adequate knowledge and skill to teach subject matter?	Weak in most areas		Adequate to do the job		Supervision knowledge and skill
Will he be likely to improve his ability to teach in the elementary school level?	Seldom seeks new methods or techniques		Modifies practices to some extent		Constantly seeking better materials, methods and techniques

SIGNATURE _____

DATE _____

190 STUDENT TEACHING: HOW, WHEN?

COLLEGE SUPERVISOR

The main responsibilty of the college supervisor is to assist the supervising teacher and the student teacher to make student teaching a successful experience. An evaluative form used by the college supervisor at the University of Georgia at Athens follows.

THE UNIVERSITY OF GEORGIA   COLLEGE OF EDUCATION

COLLEGE SUPERVISOR'S
SUMMARY-EVALUATION OF STUDENT TEACHER*

Name of Student _____ Quarter _____

School _____ Subject and/or Grade _____

Supervising Teacher _____

College Supervisor _____ Date of this Report _____

I. STUDENT TEACHER'S REPORTS:

Rate according to the following:
1. Shows good interpretation and insight into the work attempted, results achieved in terms of learning, effects upon the students, plans as to next steps, etc.
2. Indicates brief interpretations and limited insights into the work and effects of activities upon students.
3. Gives statement of work done but contains no interpretations.
4. Late report.

Weeks	1	2	3	4	5	6	7	8	9	10	11	Grade

II. OBSERVATIONS OF COLLEGE SUPERVISOR

Class observed _____

Date of observation					

*Reprinted with permission from the College of Education, University of Georgia, Athens, Georgia.

Poise					
Preparation					
Presentation					
Organization					
Pupil Reactions					
Conferences					
Rating (Total)					

Rate as follows: 1—Outstanding, 2—Above Average, 3—Average, 4—Below Average, 5—Unacceptable, N—Not Applicable

III. EVALUATION OF STUDENT TEACHER'S PERSONAL AND PROFESSIONAL PERFORMANCE

Personal and Professional Characteristics
1. Personal appearance
2. Poise and confidence
3. Voice usage
4. Enthusiasm
5. Sense of humor
6. Dependability (reliability, punctuality, etc.)
7. Adaptability
8. Initiative
9. Ability to evaluate self
10. Professional ethics
11. Relationship with other faculty members

Teaching Performance
1. Understanding of subject matter in teaching areas
2. Planning for instruction
3. Sharing with pupils the planning of instruction
4. Directing small group activities
5. Directing individual activities
6. Using teaching aids and materials
7. Understanding the individual
8. Applying principles of learning
9. Developing pupil understandings
10. Developing pupil responses

11. Developing problem-solving skills .... _____
12. Reacting to criticism .... _____
13. Word usage .... _____
14. Ability to communicate in the classroom .... _____

Classroom Organization, Management and Control
1. Establishing and using classroom routines .... _____
2. Maintaining pleasant classroom atmosphere .... _____
3. Developing group responsibilty .... _____
4. Helping pupils to establish self-control .... _____
5. Earning respect of pupils .... _____
                                                      Summary Rating _____

IV. SEMINARS GRADE: QUALITY OF PARTICIPATION .... _____

V. EXAMINATION GRADE .... _____

                Final Grades for EST 346_____ 347_____ 348_____
Rate as follows: 1—Outstanding, 2—Above Average, 3—Average,
                        4—Below Average, 5—Unacceptable, N—Not Applicable

PUPILS

Pupils can be extremely helpful in evaluating the teaching of the student teacher. Since they are constantly evaluating the teaching of the student teacher their reactions will prove valuable. The forms used for pupils' ratings of their student teachers used by Indiana University at Terre Haute and by Appalachian State University at Boone, North Carolina, follow.

INDIANA UNIVERSITY AT TERRE HAUTE

PUPIL RATING OF STUDENT TEACHER*

*Reprinted with permission from A Brief Guide to Secondary Student Teaching by Donald M. Sharpe, Division of Teaching, Indiana State University, Terre Haute, Indiana.

Pupil Rating of _____
(Name of Student Teacher)

Student teachers are anxious to learn how they may improve as teachers. Please check the statements below which you believe will be helpful to this student teacher. Be perfectly frank. You need not sign your name and you may be assured that your rating will not affect the student teacher's grade.

I. RELATIONSHIP WITH CLASS (check only one statement)
_____ Is cross, grouchy, sarcastic, mean
_____ Is unreasonable, intolerant
_____ Is pleasant, good natured, doesn't lose temper often
_____ Is kindly, practically never loses temper
_____ Is good natured, cheerful, happy, has a sense of humor

II. PRESENTATION (check only one statement)
_____ Always explains points clearly and thoroughly, easy to understand
_____ Explains so well that all but a few understand the meanings
_____ Explanations are clear and meaningful to most of the class
_____ Is understood by only a few of the best pupils
_____ Explanations are so confusing that no one understands

III. FAIRNESS (check only one statement)
_____ Treats everybody with fairness
_____ Is fair to all except the worst troublemakers
_____ Is fair to the majority of the pupils
_____ Is rather unfair to all except those who "play up" to the student teacher
_____ Is too partial, unfair; has pets

IV. CLASSROOM MANAGEMENT (check only one statement)
_____ Has no control over pupils; class is very disorderly
_____ All but a very few are disorderly
_____ Most of the class is orderly and cooperative
_____ All but a very few troublemaking students are orderly and cooperative
_____ Has excellent control over pupils; class is well-behaved and cooperative

V. PROMOTION OF INTEREST (check only one statement)
_____ Makes the subject extremely tiresome and boring
_____ Nearly all of the pupils lack interest
_____ Most of the pupils are interested
_____ All but a few of the pupils find the subject interesting
_____ Makes the subject very interesting and worthwhile to all the pupils

VI. KNOWLEDGE OF SUBJECT (check only one statement)
- _____ Knows the subject thoroughly; seldom makes a mistake
- _____ Knows the subject rather well; mistakes do not interfere with effectiveness
- _____ Generally well informed concerning the subject
- _____ Doesn't know the subject well enough; is easily confused
- _____ Doesn't know the subject; frequently makes a mistake

If you have other suggestions which you believe would help the student teacher, please add them.

APPALACHIAN STATE UNIVERSITY AT BOONE, NORTH CAROLINA

PUPIL EVALUATIVE FORM OF STUDENT TEACHER

Name of Student Teacher _____ Grade _____

Subject _____

You are asked to rate your student teacher according to the following evaluation sheet. It will in no way influence your grade, or the student teacher's grade. It is to the advantage of the student teacher to know your honest opinion of him so that he may be more conscious of his teaching techniques and adjust them accordingly. Your honest cooperation will be appreciated. Please answer the questions according to your own opinions and observations.

You Are Asked Not To Sign This Form   Rating

Trait	Poor	Average	Good
1. His voice is			
2. His dress is			
3. His cleanliness is			
4. His posture is			
5. His attitude toward you is			
6. His manners are			

*Reprinted with permission from the College of Education, Appalachian State University, Boone, North Carolina.

7. As a sport, he is ....
8. Quality of English is ....
9. His cooperation with pupils is ....
10. Pupils' cooperation with him is ....
11. His willingness to work is ....
12. Living up to his work, he is ....
13. Your respect for him as a teacher is ....
14. Your respect for him as a person is ....
15. His self-confidence is ....
16. His ability to explain is ....
17. His attention to cleanliness, lighting, ventilation, etc., of the classroom is ....
18. The bulletin boards are ....
19. His promptness in beginning class is ......
20. His ability to call pupils by name is ....
21. His provision for life-like situations is ......
22. His use of materials other than the textbook is ....
23. His preparation for class is ....
24. Your interest in this course is ....
25. Student teacher's ability to present the subject is ....
26. Student teacher's ability to arouse and hold your attention is ....
27. His encouragement of things other than subject matter is ....
28. Your feeling of ease in this classroom is ....
29. His respect for and encouragement of pupil opinion is ....

In one paragraph make any comments which will be of help to the student teacher in improving his teaching. Also make note of any exceptionally weak or strong points.

DISCUSSION NOTES

DISCUSSION NOTES

Index

Administration:
 budget, 85
 financial records, 85–86
 school aquatics, 47–48
Administrative leadership, personnel, 59–60
Adoption, budget, 84–85
Appalachian State University, 194–95
Arizona State University at Tempe, 179–82
Arnold College, 177–78
Association for Student Teaching, 15–16
Athletics, budget, 82–83, 86–87
Auxiliary gymnasium, 103

Barrow, Harold M., 154
Budget:
 adoption of budget, 84–85
 budgeting for physical education, 82–83
 expenditures, 84
 financial management, 82
 financial records, 85–86
 format, 84
 implementation of budget, 85
 interschool athletic, 86–87
 physical education, 82–83
 preparation, 83–84
 purposes, 83
 sources of income, 81–82, 84
 supplies and equipment, 87–88
Bulletin board, 103, 167

Certification, 62

Check list:
 pupil, 192–94
 supervising teacher, 182–89
Class instruction, 26
Class program:
 categories of activities, 24–25
 class instruction, 26
 guidelines for programs, 24–25
 objectives, 22–24
 philosophy, 21–22
 program activities, 25–29
 program planning, 24–25
Classroom, 109
Classroom teacher, elementary, 62
College supervisor, 4–5, 15–16, 190–92
Common terms:
 legal aspects, 138
 student teaching, 4–5
Community, 8–9
Cooperating schools:
 curriculum, 10
 facilities, 10–11
 leadership, 10
 selection, 9–10
Cooperating school administrator, 16–17
Cooperating schools, selection, 9–11
Courts area, 112–13

Demonstrations, 167
Design and construction, swimming pool, 49–50
Displays, 167

INDEX

Dressing rooms, 104–7
Drying room, 107–8

Electrical installation, 103
Elementary school, 110–12
Equipment, 87–88
Evaluation:
    competencies needed, 153–54
    criteria for selecting tests, 153
    definition, 150
    measurement, 150
    purposes of, 152
    selection of tests, 153
    types of measuring instruments, 152–53
Evaluation in student teaching:
    check lists for supervising teachers, 183–89
    college supervisor, 190
    college supervisors' evaluation, 190–92
    cooperative effort, 174
    principles, 176
    pupils, 192
    pupils' rating, 193–95
    purposes, 174, 176
    self-rating scales, 177–82
    student teacher, 177
    supervising teacher, 182
    techniques, 176–77
Expenditures, budget, 84
Extra-class program:
    extramurals, 27–28
    interscholastics, 27–29
    intramurals, 27–28
Extramurals, 27–28

Facilities, indoors:
    apparatus storage, 108
    auxiliary gymnasiums, 103
    bulletin boards, 103
    classrooms, 109
    dressing rooms, 104–8
    electrical installations, 103
    equipment drying room, 107–8
    floor space requirements, 100
    gymnasium, 100–101
    laundry room, 108
    offices, 109
    showering rooms, 104–8
    supply storage, 108
    swimming pool, 103–4
    teaching stations, 100
    team room, 107
    toilets, 107

Facilities, outdoors:
    court areas, 112
    elementary school site, 110–12
    high school boys' area, 113
    high school girls' area, 113
    interschool athletic area, 113
    junior high school site, 112–13
    planning, 109–10
    principles in planning areas, 112–13
    senior high school site, 112–13
Films, 166
Financial management, 82
Format, budget, 84
Forsythe, Charles E., 87

Gymnasium:
    finish, 101–2
    flooring, 102
    floor space, 100–101
    height, 101–2
    markings, 102
    treatment, 101–2

Income, budget, 84
Indiana University at Terre Haute, 193–94
In-service education, 62
Interscholastic athletics:
    athletics, 27–29
    budget, 86–87
Interschool athletic area, 113
Intramurals, 27–28
Iowa State University, 183–87

Knowledge and appreciation, 23

Laundry room, 108
Laws, legal aspects, 136
Legal aspects:
    defense against negligence, 140
    laws, 136
    legality of waiver, 140–41
    liability, 141
    negligence, 139–40
    paying for accidents, 138
    policies, 136
    regulations, 136
    terms used, 138
Liability, 138, 141

McGee, Rosemary, 154
Measurement, 152

INDEX 203

Measuring instruments, 152–53
Motor skills, 22–23

National Conference on Undergraduate Professional Preparation, 60–61
Negligence, 138–40
Newspapers, 165–66

Offices, 109

Permission slips, 140–41
Personnel:
   administrative leadership, 59–60
   certification, 62
   elementary classroom teachers, 62
   inservice education, 62
   physical education teachers, 60–61
   supervisory leadership, 60
Personnel roles:
   college supervisor, 15–16
   cooperating school administrator, 16–17
   student teacher, 13–14
   supervising teacher, 14–15
Philosophy, physical education, 21–22
Philosophy, student teaching, 2–11
Photographs, 166
Physical education teacher:
   competencies, 61
   qualifications, 60–61
   responsibilities, 63
Physical fitness, 22
Policies, legal aspects, 136
Posters, 167
Preparation, budget, 83–84
Program activities, 25–29
Program planning, 24–25
Public interest and support, swimming pool, 46
Public relations:
   communications with public, 164–65
   demonstrations, 167
   displays, 167
   films, 166
   functions, 162, 164
   graphics, 166
   media, 165
   newspapers, 165–66
   pictures, 166
   principles, 164
   public speeches, 166
   radio, 166
   television, 166
Pupil rating, 194–95

Radio, 166
Regulations, legal aspects, 136
Roles in student teaching:
   college supervisor, 15–16
   cooperating school administrator, 16–17
   student teacher, 12–14
   supervising teacher, 14–15

Safety:
   accidents, 126–27
   administration, 124
   curriculum, 124–25
   equipment and supplies, 125–26
   facilities, 125
   first aid, 126
   reporting accidents, 126–27
Scheduling:
   modular, 64–65
   students, 64
   teaching staff, 64
   teaching stations, 63–64
   traditional, 64
   types of, 64–65
Secondary schools, facilities:
   boys' area, 113
   courts area, 112–13
   girls' area, 113
   interschool athletic area, 113
Self-rating scale, 177–82
Sharpe, Donald M., 192
Showering rooms, 104–7
Social competence, 23–24
Sources of income, 81–82
Speeches, 166
Storage room:
   apparatus, 108
   supply, 108
Student teacher:
   characteristics of a good, 7
   role of, 13–14
   self-rating scale, 177–82
Student teaching:
   common terms, 4–5
   cooperating schools, 9–11
   evaluation, 174–94
   objectives, 5
   personnel roles, 4, 13–17
   philosophy, 3–11
   purposes, 5–7
Supervising teacher, 5, 14–15, 182–89
Supervisory leadership, personnel, 60
Supplies, 87–88
Swimming pools:
   administration of aquatics program, 47–48

Swimming Pools (*Cont.*)
  contributions of swimming, 45–46
  design and construction, 49–50
  policies and procedures, 48
  program, 47
  public support, 46

Teaching stations, 100
Team room, 107
Television, 166
Tests, selection of:
  economy, 153
  norms, 153
  objectivity, 153
  reliability, 153
  validity, 153
The Athletic Institute, 85–86, 87–88, 110
Toilets, 107
Torpey, James E., 187

University of Bridgeport, 177–78
University of Georgia, 190–92
University of Minnesota, 187–89

Waiver, 140

Situation and Analysis

Index

Budget:
    adjusting, 93–94
    approval, 89–90
    athletics, 88–89
    class instruction, 88–89
    other means of getting funds, 92–93
    purchase of supplies, 90–91
    school laundry, 91–92

Class program:
    course of study, 33
    discipline, 29–30
    excuse for ballet, 30–31
    excuse for National Guard, 33–34
    showering, 31–32
    uniforms, 32–33

Evaluation:
    communications, 156–57
    credit, 154–55
    marking, 154–55, 157–59
    physical fitness tests, 159
    tests, 155
Extra-class program:
    boxing team, 36
    eligibility standards, 36–37
    excuses for athletes, 37–38
    intramurals, 38–39
    participation on teams, 39–40

Facilities:
    dressing-showering rooms, 117–18
    folding partitions, 119
    gymnasium size and shape, 116–17
    limited, 115
    tennis courts, 115–16

Legal aspects:
    adequate facilities, 143–44
    adequate supervision, 143–44
    body contact sports, 146–47
    disciplinary measures, 141–42
    individual differences, 144
    playground apparatus, 145–46
    uniforms, 144–45

Personnel:
    classroom teachers responsibilities, 69–70
    coaches certification, 68–69
    coaching responsibilities, 67–68
    elementary physical education teachers, 70–71
    non-certified teachers, 68–69
    pupil-teacher ratio, 65–66
    pupil-teaching station ratio, 65–66
    women physical education teachers, 66–67

Public relations:
  bulletin boards, 168–69
  films, 169–70
  newspapers, 170
  parents informed, 171
  skilled performers, 167–68
  speeches, 171–72

Safety:
  floors, 131
  gymnasium apparatus, 129–30
  handicapped pupils, 131–32
  playground apparatus, 127–28
  relay races, 128–29

Safety (*Cont.*)
  sneakers, 130–31
Scheduling:
  class size, 74–75
  equitable use of facilities, 75
  factors to consider, 76
  length of class periods, 76–77
  limited facilities, 73–74
Swimming pools:
  building program, 51–52
  excuses, 55
  financing, 51
  foot baths, 54–55
  location, 53–54
  promotional information, 50–51
  sanitary conditions, 52–53

Rosenstein, Irwin